CODEX
DARK ELDAR

BY JERVIS JOHNSON
& GAVIN THORPE

Book Cover Art: David Gallagher

**Internal Art: Alexander Boyd,
Wayne England, Des Hanley,
Neil Hodgson, Nuala Kennedy,
Paul Smith, John Wigley
& Richard Wright**

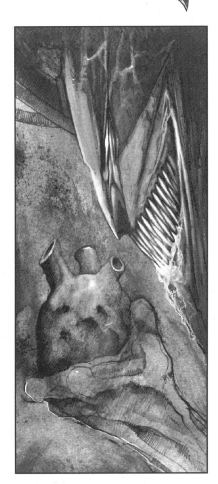

PRODUCED BY GAMES WORKSHOP

Citadel & the Citadel logo, 'Eavy Metal, Eldar, Games Workshop & the Games Workshop logo, Space Marine, Tyranid
and Warhammer are trademarks of Games Workshop Ltd registered in the UK and elsewhere in the world.
Archon, Asdrubael Vect, Beastmaster, Codex, Decapitator, Dracon, Drazhar, Grotesque, Haemonculus, Hellion, Incubi, Kruellagh the Vile,
Lelith Hesperax, Mandrake, Ork, Nob, Raider, Ravager, Reaver Jetbike, Psyker, Scourge, Succubus, Sybarite, Talos, Tech-Priest,
Urien Rakarth, Warp Beast and Wych, are all trademarks of Games Workshop Ltd.
All artwork in all Games Workshop products and the images contained therein have been produced either in-house or as work for hire.
The copyright in the artwork and the images it depicts is the exclusive property of Games Workshop Ltd.
© Copyright Games Workshop Ltd, 1998. All rights reserved.
British Cataloguing-in-Publication Data. A catalogue record for this book is available from the British Library.

UK	US	AUSTRALIA	CANADA	HONG KONG
GAMES WORKSHOP LTD.	GAMES WORKSHOP INC.	GAMES WORKSHOP,	GAMES WORKSHOP,	GAMES WORKSHOP,
WILLOW RD,	6721 BAYMEADOW DRIVE,	23 LIVERPOOL ST,	1645 BONHILL RD,	2002-2006,
LENTON,	GLEN BURNIE,	INGLEBURN,	UNITS 9-11, MISSISSAUGA,	HORIZON PLAZA,
NOTTINGHAM	MARYLAND, 21060 6401	NSW 2565	TORONTO L5T 1R3	LEE WING ST,
NG7 2WS				AP LEI CHAU

GAMES WORKSHOP®

PRODUCT CODE: 60 03 01 12 001   Games Workshop World Wide Web site: http://www.games-workshop.com   ISBN: 1-869893-41-7

INTRODUCTION

Welcome my brethren to Codex: Dark Eldar, a book entirely dedicated to collecting, painting and gaming with the most evil and decadent race in the Warhammer 40,000 universe – the Dark Eldar.

THE DARK ELDAR

The Dark Eldar inhabit a realm called Commorragh, a place as darkly twisted as its rulers, from which they launch piratical raids across the length and breadth of the Warhammer 40,000 galaxy. The purpose of these raids is not to conquer planets or protect territory, but to cause mayhem, steal and pillage, and – most important of all – capture new victims to be taken back to Commorragh. What happens to them once they arrive is best not contemplated, for if anybody in the Warhammer 40,000 universe could be called properly evil, it is the Dark Eldar. They are devious, vain and totally self-serving, with no respect for any living creature, not even themselves. They revel in inflicting pain and suffering, and glory in causing death and destruction. The Dark Eldar are not nice, not nice at all, and to be captured by them is a fate far worse than death!

WHY COLLECT A DARK ELDAR ARMY?

In the right hands the Dark Eldar are a deadly foe, but make no mistake, they are not an easy army to use. Other armies can rely on nice thick armour or large numbers of models to cope with their leader's errors of judgement, but not the Dark Eldar. The troops that make up a Dark Eldar army are quite fragile, and it takes cunning and guile to use them well. However, if you possess the finesse and skill, a Dark Eldar army can run rings around any enemy, leaving them bloody, terrified, and, most importantly of all, totally defeated!

Three things typify the Dark Eldar army: it's very fast, has lots of firepower, and is lightly armoured. Most Dark Eldar infantry can move faster than any other troops apart from their cousins, the Craftworld Eldar. With their access to a large number of Raider transports, the Dark Eldar possess an unprecedented level of mobility. They also utilise an impressive array of sophisticated heavy weapons, which allow them to lay down a withering hail of fire. However, they do not possess any tanks, and with the exception of a very limited number of Incubi and Talos, don't have any heavily armoured troops. The result is an army that rewards a player who can use it with subtlety and cunning, but which will punish the player who simply hurls it headlong into battle.

Of course battlefield effectiveness is not the only reason for collecting an army, and the Dark Eldar have a lot to offer a player who is looking for an army with a certain flair. The army includes a wide variety of very different models, and this makes it possible to collect a really individual force with its own unique style. The appearance of the army is exceptional too: the Dark Eldar model range, combined with the brooding look that epitomises the army, creates a force that looks as great on the shelf as it does on the battlefield. As you can see, in just about every way the Dark Eldar are a connoisseur's army!

WHAT'S IN THIS BOOK

This book breaks down into the following three main sections:

The Army List. This tells you about the different characters, troops, weapons and vehicles available to a Dark Eldar army, and how to work out an army for use in a Warhammer 40,000 game.

Painting and Collecting Guide. Describes choosing an army, basic tactics plus step by step details of assembling and painting models and vehicles. This section also shows examples of Dark Eldar colour schemes and markings, gives advice on choosing your own schemes, and tips on modelling and converting.

The Dark Eldar. The final section is dedicated to background details and extra information about the Dark Eldar.

They are not your worst nightmare; they are your every nightmare.

Colonel Brynner gazed numbly at the display screen, his fingers tapping on his thigh in agitation. The dark icons representing the Eldar raiders were quickly encircling his forces who were guarding the command tower. More and more of the blue icons of his army flickered and then disappeared as units failed to report in and were presumed destroyed. The situation was looking hopeless; comm-link orders were becoming difficult to issue as more and more comm-channels were filled with gibbering cries of terror and torment. The Eldar attack was fluid, ever-changing, and impossible to muster a force against in one place. Snapping out of his dazed state, the Colonel strode to the armourglas window and looked out. The cold, clinical icons of the strategic display did little justice to the horrific scene that greeted him.

Like a swarm of ravening beasts, the Eldar were spilling across the plains. Waves of jetbikes moved rapidly from one defensive position to the next, swiftly over-running the beleaguered Imperial forces. Around them hovered swarms of Eldar warriors mounted on one-man anti-grav craft, darting in and around the main enemy squads to harry the retreating forces and sow confusion and anarchy. The larger shapes of the Eldar transports and heavy weapons vehicles glided effortlessly through the darkening sky, pulses of energy lighting up the twilight of dusk. Wherever the Eldar attacked, a ragged stream of Guardsmen fled back towards the command complex. Many of them were quickly run down by the swift Eldar and piles of human corpses littered the approaches to the citadel.

As night rapidly fell, the automatic searchlights lit up, bathing the battlefield in roving columns of light. For Brynner, this only added to the sense of unreal nightmare, as shadowy shapes flitted through the beams, the pulse of weapons erupted across the ebon horizon and the Eldar moved ever closer. Within minutes the perimeter alarms were wailing, notifying the defenders of a breach in the outer wall. The defensive batteries opened fire, shaking the command tower with the recoil of fifty guns firing in unison, cutting a swathe through the onslaught of the Eldar. However, the Eldar responded with even more ferocity. Thin rays of black light, seen only as they cut through the searchlight's beams, picked out the guns in turn, systematically eliminating the control bunker's armaments. The searchlights were the next target and within a few heartbeats the only light to be seen was the pale glimmering aura of interior lights shining through vision slits.

An explosion rocked the bunker, and the lanterns inside flickered and failed as the energy grid shut down. The bunker was plunged into darkness for half a minute before the back-up systems came on-line and lit the inside of the bastion with their ruddy glow. All the while, the comm-net was full of the shouts of desperate soldiers, the screams of the wounded and the gibbering of men driven insane with terror. Another klaxon sounded, low and ominous, and one of the command staff reported the outer doors had been breached – the Eldar were inside the building.

Switching his gaze to the internal viewers, Brynner watched the progress of the aliens' attack, as they ran down corridors, unleashing hails of deadly fire from their exotic weapons. His men were falling back steadily, the survivors were hardened to the wiles of the foe now; resigned to their deaths they were selling their lives as dearly as possible. It was pointless though, the Eldar shot and cut down men by the score. At the forefront were heavily-armoured warriors with gleaming power weapons. Compared to the ruthless barbarity of the other Eldar, these warriors advanced in a cool, detached fashion, mercilessly dispatching anyone who stood in their path. Brynner saw Commissar Helsreich cut in half with one blow from a massive powered glaive, his bodyguard of Storm Troopers slaughtered with equal ease. It was only then that Brynner realised that the Eldar were scant moments from reaching the control room. Turning to Veriax, the Tech-Priest, he straightened his back and took a deep breath.

"Erinyes Station is lost. Prepare the plasma reactor for critical overload. We'll not let them take us alive..."

Subject Cipher: Reaver. Subject Classification: Jetcycle. Subject Origin: Eldar [Pirate]

Ref: DE/2626/a

File: S - D345

Received: Imp 57458

Source: 1 (higher)

Data: Classified

Date: 1848576.M41

Order: Retorum

γ

α

Subject Description: The Reaver Jetcycle is a one-crew vehicle employing anti-gravitic impulse. The anti-gravitic generator is highly advanced, housed within the structure of the vehicle just beneath the rider's position. It is propelled forward by a sophisticated combustive jet which utilises a fuel source as yet unknown to our Tech-Adepts. The bulk of the Jetcycle appears to be of variable configuration. The frontal canopy, rear canards and keel blade are all capable of assuming various forms. Whether this is for aesthetic reasons, some kind of control mechanism or just to alter the vehicle's combat performance in different battlefield situations, it is impossible to tell. As you can see from the combat data display in the image below, the Reaver Jetcycle is capable of very high speeds, using a secondary booster to propel itself forward at an astounding rate for short periods of time. Primary armament is of standard Eldar pirate design, firing a hail of splinter-like ammunition, often coated with toxic substances. Occasionally this is replaced by different weapons [crossfile/Eldar Blaster & Eldar Shredder]. Although mounting a ranged weapon, the favoured method of attack appears to be close combat, using the rapidity of the Reaver to close quickly, slashing at foes with the cycle's blades as the attacker swoops past. Post-battle reports have shown that the riders of these vehicles are highly skilled at this type of attack, able to disembowel an opponent, sever a limb, or even attain such an accurate attack run that the caratoid artery or jugular vein is severed during the pass.

[Status: Deviant Escaping]   Rectify Aim: 0/6°/98

Grid: 86/A/92
Time: 1/44: %/A
Vector: 6°/44
Speed: 258K/F

Cross file: AD/I/81/7
Image Source: Adeptus Astartes Dreadnought; Delta 9 Massacre

"For many Imperial Commanders the form of warfare employed by the Dark Eldar is difficult to grasp and therefore to counter. Whereas the duty of the Imperial Commander is either to seize or defend territory, the Dark Eldar make war only to steal. If, as a by-product of this, they are able to indulge their vile passion for murder, torture and other decadent acts, then they will joyfully do so, but this is not their primary goal. Dark Eldar tactics, therefore, revolve around the desire to seize that which they want, and then to escape with it. They are the masters of the surprise attack, and will rarely attack a target they know is well defended or prepared. It almost goes without saying that the Dark Eldar will use stealth and guile to win that which they desire, rather than a simple head-on attack. The vehicles and weapons the Dark Eldar use are all well suited to the tasks for which they are employed; Dark Eldar Jetbikes and Raiders allow for the rapid movement and redeployment of their troops, while the weapons they use are designed primarily to lay down a heavy, short-ranged fire that can subdue an enemy as much by its intensity as its effect. Although lightly armed and armoured (at least by the standards of our own forces), the Dark Eldar are swift, and will generally attempt to use their mobility to avoid an opponent's main strength. As can be seen, in all ways the Dark Eldar are the masters of the tactics of the raider, the pirate and the bandit, and in no way show any desire to follow the noble calling of the true warrior or soldier. Yet, although they should rightly be despised for using such ignoble tactics, they should never be under-estimated, for to do so will undoubtably lead to defeat and death.

Taken from "The Dark Eldar: Their Methods And How To Defeat Them, By One Who Has Done So", Colonel Schifflen Van Dyson,
7th Vangrian Royal Guard. All printings suppressed by order of the Administratum, M0150935.M32.
Sole remaining copy maintained as Inquisition Record INR 1345/H46

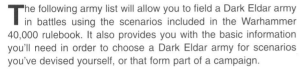
The following army list will allow you to field a Dark Eldar army in battles using the scenarios included in the Warhammer 40,000 rulebook. It also provides you with the basic information you'll need in order to choose a Dark Eldar army for scenarios you've devised yourself, or that form part of a campaign.

The army list is split into five sections: *Headquarters (HQ)*, *Elites*, *Troops*, *Fast Attack* and *Heavy Assault*. All of the squads, vehicles and characters in the army are placed into one of these depending upon their role on the battlefield. In addition, every model in the army is given a points value which varies depending upon how effective the model is on the battlefield.

Before you choose an army you will need to agree with your opponent which scenario you will be fighting and the total number of points each of you will spend on your armies. Having done this you can proceed to pick an army as described below.

FORCE ORGANISATION CHARTS

The army lists are used in conjunction with the force organisation chart from a scenario. Each chart is split into five categories that correspond to the sections in the army list, and each category may have one or more boxes. Each light toned box means that you **may make one** choice from that section of the army list, but a dark toned box means that you **must** make a choice from that section of the army list.

Note that unless a model or vehicle forms part of a squad or a squadron, it is a single choice from what is available to your army.

STANDARD MISSIONS

COMPULSORY	OPTIONAL
1 HQ	1 HQ
2 Troops	3 Elites
	4 Troops
	3 Fast Attack
	3 Heavy Support

The Standard Missions force organisation chart is a good example of how to choose your army. To begin with you will need at least one HQ unit and two Troop units (dark shaded boxes indicate units that must be taken). This leaves the following options for you to choose from to make up your army's total points value: up to 1 HQ unit, 0-3 additional Elite units, 0-4 additional Troop units, 0-3 additional Fast Attack units or 0-3 additional Heavy Support units.

USING THE ARMY LISTS

To make a choice, look in the relevant section in the army list and decide what unit you want, how many models there can be in it, and what upgrades you want (if any). Remember that you cannot field models that are equipped with weapons and wargear if they are not shown on the model. Then, simply subtract the points cost of the unit from your total points, and go back and make another choice. Continue doing this until you have spent all your points.

ARMY LIST ENTRIES

Each army list entry consists of the following:

Unit Name: The type of unit and any limitations (if any) on the maximum number of choices you can make for it (eg 0-1).

Profile: These are the characteristics of that unit type, including its points cost. Where the unit has different warriors, there may be more than one profile.

Number/Squad: The number of models allowed in the unit, or the number of models you may take for one choice from the force organisation chart. Often this is a variable amount, in which case it shows the minimum and maximum unit size.

Weapons: These are the unit's standard weapons.

Options: Lists the different weapon/equipment options for the unit and any additional points cost for taking them. It may also include the option to upgrade a squad member to a character. If a squad is allowed to have models with upgraded weaponry (eg, heavy weapons, shredders, etc) then these may only be taken by ordinary squad members, not the character.

Special Rules: This is where you'll find any special rules that apply to the unit.

SPECIAL RULES

Fleet of Foot

The Dark Eldar are a lithe and agile race, noted for their fleetness of foot. In the shooting phase you may declare that a Dark Eldar unit is going to run instead of shoot. Roll a D6. The result is the distance the unit may move in that shooting phase. This move is not affected by difficult terrain or any other movement restrictions.

The following models may not run:

- Dark Eldar vehicles or jetbikes
- Any model with a saving throw better than 4+, eg Incubi
- Talos or Grotesques
- Hellions or Scourges

Piratical Raiders

The type of Dark Eldar army represented by this list is a raiding force, intent on making a swift attack, seizing prisoners etc, and then escaping as quickly as possible. It's not the kind of force used to capture and hold territory against enemy attacks. To represent this, in any mission where there is an attacker and a defender, the Dark Eldar are always the attackers.

Capturing Prisoners

The Dark Eldar almost always take prisoners during their raids. What happens to them is best not even contemplated. So, if the Dark Eldar win a close combat and force their opponents to fall back, roll a D6 for each enemy casualty in the assault. On a 4+, the model is taken as a prisoner. In addition, if the Dark Eldar advance and destroy their opponents by moving further than them, any enemy models removed are captured rather than killed. Place all captured models to one side. At the end of the mission each captured model is worth 1 victory point to the Dark Eldar player. In missions where victory points are not used prisoners have no effect on the outcome of the battle, but it's great for the Dark Eldar player to know just how many 'poor, unfortunate souls' he is going to take back.

DARK ELDAR ARMOURY

Characters may be given up to two single-handed weapons, or a single-handed weapon and a two-handed weapon. In addition, you can also pick 100 points worth of wargear for each character but no model can have the same item of wargear more than once.

All wargear and weapons chosen must be represented on the model.

SINGLE-HANDED WEAPONS

Agoniser	20 pts
Close combat weapon	1 pt
Destructor (Haemonculi only)	15 pts
Poisoned blades	5 pts
Power weapon	15 pts
Scissorhand (Haemonculi only)	5 pts
Splinter pistol	1 pt
Stinger (Haemonculi only)	5 pts

TWO-HANDED WEAPONS

Hellglaive (no other weapons may be used)	5 pts
Punisher (no other weapons may be used)	20 pts
Splinter rifle	2 pts

WARGEAR

Crucible of Malediction (no more than one per army)	20 pts
Combat drugs	25 pts
Gruesome talisman	2 pts
Haywire grenades	4 pts
Hell mask	5 pts
Hellion skyboard	15 pts
Reaver jetbike	35 pts
Plasma grenades	2 pts
Shadow field (no more than one per army)	25 pts
Soul seeker ammunition	10 pts
Terrorfex	15 pts
Tormentor helm	5 pts
Trophy rack	5 pts
Webway portal	50 pts

HQ

DARK ELDAR LORD

	Points	WS	BS	S	T	W	I	A	Ld	Sv
Archon	60	6	6	3	3	3	7	3	9	5+
Dracon	35	5	5	3	3	2	6	2	9	5+

Options: The Dark Eldar Lord can be given any equipment allowed from the Dark Eldar Armoury.

SPECIAL RULES

Independent Character: Unless accompanied by a Retinue (see below) the Dark Eldar Lord is an independent character and follows the Independent Character special rules as given in the Warhammer 40,000 rulebook.

Retinue: The Dark Eldar Lord may be accompanied by a retinue of his finest warriors. These may either be Dark Eldar Warriors and/or Incubi, as described in the Retinue entry below. If the Lord has a Retinue then he and the Retinue are treated as a single unit during battle. Note that the Retinue does not count as a separate HQ choice (it does not use up one of the HQ 'slots').

Dark Eldar thrive on domination and power, and those who are vicious and ruthless enough will quickly rise to positions of authority. The Dark Eldar Lords lead their servants into battle in the search for slaves and souls, leaving worlds in ruin and a veritable mountain of dead heaped in their wake.

HAEMONCULUS

	Points/Model	WS	BS	S	T	W	I	A	Ld	Sv
Haemonculus	25	4	4	3	4	2	4	2	8	5+

Number: You may include between one and three Haemonculi as a single HQ choice.

Options: Each Haemonculus may be given equipment from the Dark Eldar Armoury. They can be given wargear normally, but are restricted to 'Haemonculi only' weapons.

SPECIAL RULES

Independent Character: Each Haemonculus is an independent character and follows the Independent Character special rules as given in the Warhammer 40,000 rulebook.

There is no pain unknown to the Haemonculi, no agony they cannot administer upon their victims. They treat the infliction of misery and death as the highest of arts, gleefully producing choruses of screams and taking delight in every nuance of discomfort and woe.

DARK ELDAR RETINUE

	Points/Model	WS	BS	S	T	W	I	A	Ld	Sv
Warrior	8	4	4	3	3	1	5	1	8	5+
Incubi	25	5	4	3	3	1	5	1	8	3+
Incubi Master	+18	5	4	3	3	1	6	2	9	3+

If your army has a Dark Eldar Lord it may also have a Retinue. See the Dark Eldar Lord entry above.

Squad: The Retinue contains between five and ten Dark Eldar (either Warriors and/or Incubi).

Weapons: Dark Eldar Warriors are armed with splinter rifles. Incubi are armed with a tormentor helm and a punisher.

Options: Up to two Dark Eldar Warriors may be armed with either a splinter cannon at +10 pts each or a dark lance at +15 pts each. Up to two Incubi may be armed with a shredder at +10 pts each or a blaster at +6 pts each.

Character: If the Retinue consists of five or more Incubi, one of them may be upgraded to an Incubi Master for +18 pts. The Master is armed with a tormentor helm and a punisher and may have any additional wargear allowed from the Dark Eldar Armoury.

Raider: If the Dark Eldar Lord and his Retinue number ten models or less they may be mounted on a Raider at an additional cost of +55 pts. See the Troops section of this army list for details of the Raider.

A Retinue is made up of the Dark Eldar Lord's most trusted (and deadliest!) servants. The Retinue will protect their Lord in battle, but, as the Dark Eldar are an evil and power-hungry race, a Lord requires a Retinue to also protect him from his own followers nearly as much as they are required to shield him from the enemy!

ELITES

GROTESQUES

	Points/Model	WS	BS	S	T	W	I	A	Ld	Sv
Grotesque	15	4	0	4	3	2	3	2	5	none

Squad: The squad consists of between three and ten Grotesques.

Weapons: None.

Raider: If a squad of Grotesques is accompanied by an independent character they may be mounted in a Raider at an additional cost of +55 pts. The independent character must be purchased as a separate HQ choice, and must accompany the Grotesques in order to get them to mount or dismount from the Raider.

SPECIAL RULES

Stupid: Grotesques are not noted for their intelligence. Unless accompanied by an independent character they must pass a Leadership test in order to move in the movement phase. They do not need to test in order to make an assault move.

Feel No Pain: Grotesques are inured to pain and shrug off minor wounds that would leave another creature writhing in agony. Because of this they ignore shooting hits from weapons whose Strength is not at least twice the Grotesque's Toughness (ie, they are only affected by shooting weapons with a Strength of 6+). This means that ranged attacks that can affect Grotesques will always get an outright kill (you either kill them outright or not at all – no half measures!). Note that hits in close combat affect the Grotesque normally (as you can chop bits off them!).

Terrifying Opponent: Grotesques are horrible opponents to fight against. Any opponent beaten by them in close combat automatically falls back without a Leadership test being taken.

All Dark Eldar take pleasure in suffering, especially in the infliction of pain. There are some who have become so obsessed by this need for torture that they have even turned upon their own bodies. Others are less voluntary about their twisted, manipulated flesh, having fallen victim to the attention of the Haemonculi through some real or perceived misdeed, or by simply being in the wrong place at the wrong time.

MANDRAKES

	Points/Model	WS	BS	S	T	W	I	A	Ld	Sv
Mandrake	15	4	4	3	3	1	5	1	8	5+

Squad: A Mandrake squad consists of between five and ten Mandrakes.

Weapons: Splinter pistol and close combat weapon.

SPECIAL RULES

Shadow-skinned: The special chameleon-like qualities of the Mandrakes allow them to blend into the background, even when standing in open terrain. Mandrakes always count as being in cover, giving them a 5+ saving throw against most attacks. This counts in an assault as well, so unless the attackers are armed with frag grenades, the Mandrakes will always strike first. If attacked by something that ignores cover their normal armour save of 5+ applies.

Hidden Deployment: Mandrakes are not deployed like other troops. They are always deployed at the start of the battle, even if the mission's special rules say they must be held in reserve. However, instead of placing the unit on the table as normal, take three Mandrake models (no matter how many models are in the squad), and deploy them separately in any place allowed by the deployment rules for the mission. Any one of these models can represent the actual location of the Mandrake squad, though you don't have to decide which one until the squad is revealed.

Until the squad's location is revealed your opponent may not shoot, assault, or otherwise attack the Mandrakes in any way, but, by the same token, the Mandrakes do not affect the enemy, and can't be used for crossfire purposes, to block lines of sight, etc. All that the individual models may do is move up to 6" in the movement phase. They can do nothing else, and may not make a *fleet of foot* move instead of shooting.

You may reveal the true location of the squad at the start of any phase during your own turn. However, you must have revealed their location by the end of the third turn. Pick one of the Mandrake models, and remove all the others from the table, then deploy the rest of the squad within 4" of the model you picked. Once revealed, the Mandrakes follow the normal rules and may not return to 'hidden' status again during the game.

Mandrakes are the most malevolent of the Dark Eldar, preying on their own kind from the shadows of Commorragh. Who can say how a Dark Eldar Lord can entice these vile creatures to serve him in battle. What prizes can be offered to beasts who crave flesh and blood and little else?

WYCHES

	Points/Model	WS	BS	S	T	W	I	A	Ld	Sv
Wyches	10	4	4	3	3	1	0	1	8	0+
Wych Succubus	+8	4	4	3	3	1	6	2	8	6+

Squad: The squad consists of between five and twenty Wyches.

Weapons: Splinter pistol and close combat weapon.

Options: Up to two models may be armed with a shredder at +10 pts or a blaster at +5 pts. All models in the squad may be armed with plasma grenades at +2 pts per model and/or haywire grenades at +4 pts per model. One Wych model may be armed with a shardnet and impaler, one model may be armed with hydraknives and another Wych model may be armed with a razorsnare and falchion, all at no additional points cost.

Character: One of the Wych models can be upgraded to a Wych Succubus at an additional cost of +8 pts. The Wych Succubus is armed with a splinter pistol & close combat weapon, or with one of the three Wych weapon combinations from the list below. The Wych Succubus may also choose extra equipment from the Armoury.

Raider: If the squad has ten or less models they can be mounted on a Raider at an extra cost of +55 pts.

SPECIAL RULES

Combat Drugs: Wyches use combat drugs to artificially boost their already finely honed abilities. Roll a D6 for each Wych squad at the start of the battle to see what effect the vile narcotics have on the unit. The effect lasts for the entire battle. If the Wych Succubus leading the squad has a combat drug dispenser then its effects only apply to them and replace the effects of the squad's own evil concoctions.

D6	Result
1	May make a 12" assault move and a 3D6" pursuit or fall back move.
2	+1 WS
3	+1 S
4	Always strikes first
5	Re-roll any misses in close combat.
6	+1 Attack

Wych Weapons:

Shardnet and impaler: The shardnet is used to ensnare or distract opponents, so that they suffer a -1 to hit modifier. The impaler allows the Wych to always strike first in the first round of combat, even against opponents in cover. The model counts as having two close combat weapons and receives a +1 Attack in close combat.

Hydraknives: A Wych armed with a pair of hydraknives always strikes last in close combat but doubles its Attacks after any modifiers have been applied. The model counts as having two close combat weapons and receives a +1 Attack in close combat.

Razorsnare and Falchion: The falchion is a special type of blade that counts as a close combat weapon. When combined with the razorsnare, it gives a +1 Attack bonus as a second weapon. The razorsnare allows the Wych to 'pull' a model who is within 2" into base contact. In addition, opponents fighting a Wych who has a razorsnare lose the benefit of using two close combat weapons (ie, they don't get the +1 Attack they would normally receive).

Ruled over by their Succubi, Wyches spend their entire lives perfecting the skills of gladiatorial combat. Few survive their first duel, but those who live learn quickly. A Dark Eldar Lord with sufficient means can hire these highly-skilled warriors to accompany him into battle, promising great rewards for those whose fighting displays are most pleasing to watch.

If you have any squads of Wyches in your army you may take one pack of Warp Beasts. The Warp Beasts are a separate unit, but do not count as a separate Elites choice with regard to the number of Elite units you may have in the army.

0-1 WARP BEAST PACK

	Points/Model	WS	BS	S	T	W	I	A	Ld	Sv
Warp Beast	12	4	0	4	3	1	5	3	3	6+
Beastmaster	15	4	4	3	3	1	6	1	8	6+

Squad: The pack consists of a Beastmaster and between three and five Warp Beasts.

Weapons: The Beastmaster is armed with an agoniser and a splinter pistol. The Warp Beasts must rely on their razor-sharp teeth and claws!

SPECIAL RULES

Warp Beasts: Warp Beasts are incredibly fast, even by Dark Eldar standards. They count as being *fleet of foot*, and may charge up to 12" in the assault phase in the same way as cavalry do. Warp Beasts move through difficult terrain just like infantry. If they move through difficult terrain whilst they are assaulting, they move equal to double the highest dice roll. If the Beastmaster is slain and the pack are forced to fall back, they will return to the warp, and are removed from play.

Beastmaster: Beastmasters are a subset of the Wych cult that fight against wild creatures in the arenas of Commorragh. They use combat drugs like Wyches, but always receive the 12" assault move result, in order to allow them to keep up with their pack. If the Beastmaster is slain then the pack will move towards the nearest unit (friend or foe) in the Dark Eldar turn, and assault them if they can.

Spawned from the bloody nightmares of mortals, Warp Beasts are death and pain embodied. They are voracious predators who will attack anything they can find. It is the task of the Beastmasters to catch these creatures; fight against them in the arena or guide them into battle and unleash them upon the unwitting foe!

TROOPS

Dark Eldar Warriors attack rapidly, killing or crippling those who oppose them. They then drag off any survivors back to Commorragh to be tortured and killed at leisure.

WARRIOR SQUAD

	Points/Model	WS	BS	S	T	W	I	A	Ld	Sv
Warrior	8	4	4	3	3	1	5	1	8	5+
Sybarite	+6	4	4	3	3	1	5	2	8	5+

Squad: The squad consists of between ten and twenty Dark Eldar Warriors.

Weapons: Splinter rifle.

Options: Up to two models may be armed with a shredder at +10 pts or a blaster at +5 pts.

Up to two models in the squad may be armed with either a dark lance or a splinter cannon at +10 pts.

Character: One Dark Eldar Warrior may be upgraded to a Sybarite at an additional cost of +6 pts. The Sybarite is armed with either a splinter rifle or a splinter pistol and a close combat weapon, and may choose additional equipment from the Dark Eldar Armoury.

Dark Eldar are technologically highly advanced, as evinced by their sleek, fast Raiders. Squads mounted on Raiders sweep about the battlefield, darting swiftly from one fight to the next, never staying still long enough for the enemy to bring sufficient force forward to destroy them.

RAIDER SQUAD

	Points/Model	WS	BS	S	T	W	I	A	Ld	Sv
Warrior	8	4	4	3	3	1	5	1	8	5+
Sybarite	+6	4	4	3	3	1	5	2	8	5+

Squad: The squad consists of between five and ten Dark Eldar Warriors mounted on a Raider (see the Raider option below for details).

Weapons: Splinter rifle.

Options: Up to one model may be armed with a shredder at +10 pts or a blaster at +5 pts.

Up to one model in the squad may be armed with either a dark lance or a splinter cannon at +10 pts.

Character: One of the Dark Eldar may be upgraded to a Sybarite at an additional cost of +6 pts. The Sybarite is armed with a splinter rifle or a splinter pistol and close combat weapon, and may choose additional equipment from the Dark Eldar Armoury.

Raider: The squad must be mounted on a Raider at an additional cost of +55 pts.

The Dark Eldar strike rapidly from their ships and warp portals, descending upon the enemy on their sleek Raiders. Utilising a grasp of anti-grav technology far more sophisticated than any other race, the Raiders allow the Dark Eldar to attack savagely into the heart of the enemy, giving them little chance to react or muster a defence.

Transport: RAIDER

	Points	Front Armour	Side Armour	Rear Armour	BS
Raider	55	10	10	10	4

Type: Skimmer, fast, open-topped

Crew: Dark Eldar Warriors

Weapons: The Raider is armed with a dark lance.

Options: The dark lance may be upgraded to a disintegrator at a cost of +5 pts.

Transport: The Raider may transport up to ten Dark Eldar.

FAST ATTACK

REAVER JETBIKE SQUAD

	Points/Model	WS	BS	S	T	W	I	A	Ld	Sv
Reaver	30	4	4	4	4	1	6	1	8	4+
Reaver Succubus	+16	4	4	4	4	1	6	2	8	4+

Squad: The squad consists of between three and ten Reaver jetbikes.

Weapons: The Reaver jetbike rider is armed with a splinter pistol and the jetbike is fitted with a splinter rifle.

Options: Up to two bikes can replace their splinter rifles with a shredder at +15 pts or a blaster at +10 pts.

Character: One rider may be upgraded to a Reaver Succubus at an additional cost of +16 pts. The Reaver Succubus may choose additional equipment from the Dark Eldar Armoury.

SPECIAL RULES

Reaver Jetbike: Special rules apply to the Reaver jetbike. These are included in the Wargear section of this Codex.

Combat Drugs: Reaver jetbike riders are a subset of the Wych cult, and like them they use combat drugs to artificially boost their abilities. Roll a D6 for each Reaver jetbike squad at the start of the battle to see what effect the vile narcotics have on the unit. A separate D6 roll is made for each unit, and the effect lasts for the entire battle. If the Reaver Succubus leading the squad is given a combat drug dispenser then its effects only apply to them and replace the effects of the squad's own evil concoctions.

D6	Result
1	Crazed! Ignores fall back results of any type, always advances after a combat and never consolidates.
2	+1 WS
3	+1 S
4	Always strikes first
5	Re-roll any misses in close combat.
6	+1 Attack

Fear the shadows; despise the night. There are horrors that no man can face and live.

0-1 HELLIONS

	Points/Model	WS	BS	S	T	W	I	A	Ld	Sv
Hellion	16	4	4	3	3	1	6	1	8	5+
Hellion Succubus	+16	4	4	3	3	1	6	2	8	5+

Squad: The squad consists of between three and ten Hellions.

Weapons: Each Hellion is armed with a hellglaive.

Options: Up to one Hellion may be armed with a shredder at +15 pts or a blaster at +10 pts.

Character: One Hellion may be upgraded to a Hellion Succubus at an additional cost of +16 pts. The Hellion Succubus may choose additional equipment from the Dark Eldar Armoury.

SPECIAL RULES

Hellion skyboard & hellglaive: Special rules apply to the Hellion skyboard and hellglaive. These are included in the Wargear section of this Codex.

Combat Drugs: Hellions are a subset of the Wych cult, and like Wyches they use combat drugs to artificially boost their abilities. Roll a D6 for each Hellion squad at the start of the battle to see what effect the vile narcotics have on the unit. A separate D6 roll is made for each unit, and the effect lasts for the entire battle. If the Hellion Succubus leading the squad is given a combat drug dispenser then its effects only apply to them and replace the effects of the squad's own evil concoctions.

D6	Result
1	Crazed! Ignores all fall back results, always advances after a combat and never consolidates.
2	+1 WS
3	+1 S
4	Always strikes first
5	Re-roll any misses in close combat.
6	+1 Attack

Riding ultra-fast jetbikes, Reavers combine speed with excellent skill at close quarter fighting, they race ahead of the main Dark Eldar attack, slicing through enemy squads without pause.

Mounted on multi-bladed skyboards, Hellions sweep down from the sky screaming chilling battle cries. They delight in surprise attacks, using their speed and specialised weapons to strike quick and hard, and then move out of range before the enemy can turn their guns on them.

"I will never forget what I saw at Obsidian Station. The bones of five thousand brave men lay scattered about the winding corridors. Their blood was slick upon the walls and floors of the dormitories. Their innards were hung from control panels like grotesque decorations of some insane celebration. But not a single skull was to be found; taken as sick trophies by these despicable attackers."

Inquisitor Absolvus

HEAVY SUPPORT

A On black pinions, Scourges drop down from the skies, their heavy weapons unleashing a hail of splinters and pulses of dark energy. They attack wherever they please, and strike where least expected, utilising their wings to quickly retreat or drive forward depending upon the enemy's strength.

A Ravagers are variants of the Raider. Mounting a deadly battery of heavy weaponry, they have been the bane of tanks and other vehicles across the galaxy. Combining amazing speed with awesome weaponry, they can easily outmanoeuvre and blow apart the lumbering vehicles of other races.

A Constructed by the insane Haemonculi, the Talos is a torture device that sweeps across the battlefield on anti-gravitic motors, latching on to its foes and incarcerating them within its armoured shell. The death spasms of those captured propel the Talos towards its enemies as its unique Sting wildly spews death in all directions and its many-bladed arms cut through armour and bone with lashing blows.

DARK ELDAR SCOURGES

	Points/Model	WS	BS	S	T	W	I	A	Ld	Sv
Scourge	16	4	4	3	3	1	5	1	8	5+
Sybarite	+6	4	4	3	3	1	5	2	8	5+

Squad: The squad consists of between five and ten Dark Eldar Scourges.

Weapons: Splinter rifles.

Options: Up to four Dark Eldar Scourges may be armed with splinter cannons at +20 pts or dark lances at an additional cost of +25 pts.

Character: One of the Dark Eldar Scourges may be upgraded to a Sybarite at an additional cost of +6 pts. The Sybarite may be armed with a splinter rifle or a splinter pistol and close combat weapon, and may be given additional equipment from the Dark Eldar Armoury.

SPECIAL RULES

Jump Packs: Scourges' wings work in the same way as jump packs.

Deep Strike: Scourges can reach almost anywhere on the battlefield. To represent this they can enter play as reserves using the *Deep Strike* rules given in the Warhammer 40,000 rulebook, even in missions where reserves and *Deep Strike* cannot normally be used.

RAVAGER

	Points	Front Armour	Side Armour	Rear Armour	BS
Ravager	105	11	11	10	4

Type: Skimmer, fast, open-topped.   **Crew:** Dark Eldar Warriors.

Weapons: The Ravager is armed with three dark lances.

Options: Any of the dark lances may be upgraded to a disintegrator at a cost of +5 pts each.

TALOS

	Points/Model	WS	BS	S	T	W	I	A	Ld	Sv
Talos	100	5	3	7	7	3	4	D6	–	3+

Weapons: The Talos is armed with a Talos sting and Talos claws.

SPECIAL RULES

Talos Sting: This is a unique weapon found only on the Talos. It has the following profile.

Range 24"	Strength 4	AP 5	Assault 6

Wildfire: A Talos fires off wild volleys of shots rather than aiming at a specific target. When it shoots, roll to hit as normal. Then allocate the first hit scored to the nearest enemy model to the Talos, the second hit to the second closest model, and so on until all the hits (if there are any!) have been used up. Note that this may mean that models from different units are hit by the attacks. Also note that only models within range of the weapon and in its line of sight can be hit. Once all possible targets in range and within its line of sight have been hit once each, any further hits are wasted.

Talos Claws: The Talos gets D6 attacks with its claws (+1 if charging) when it fights in close combat. Roll to hit and wound normally. No armour saves are allowed against the claws. Against a vehicle roll only once for Armour penetration, but add +1 to the Armour Penetration dice roll for each hit scored by the Talos after the first (eg, if the Talos hits a vehicle three times with its claws it would add +2 to its AP roll).

Fearless: The Talos never falls back and cannot be pinned. It is automatically assumed to pass any morale checks.

Skimmer: The Talos can move over difficult terrain without penalty. However, if it starts or finishes its move in difficult terrain it will suffer a wound with no save on a D6 roll of 1.

DARK ELDAR SUMMARY

	WS	BS	S	T	W	I	A	Ld	Sv
Archon	6	6	3	3	3	7	3	9	5+
Dracon	5	5	3	3	2	6	2	9	5+
Haemonculus	4	4	3	4	2	4	2	8	5+
Incubi Master	5	4	3	3	1	6	2	9	3+
Incubi	5	4	3	3	1	5	1	8	3+
Grotesque	4	0	4	3	2	3	2	5	n/a
Wych	4	4	3	3	1	6	1	8	6+
Wych Succubus	4	4	3	3	1	6	2	8	6+
Warp Beast	4	0	4	3	1	5	3	3	6+
Beastmaster	4	4	3	3	1	6	1	8	6+
Mandrake	4	4	3	3	1	5	1	8	5+
Sybarite	4	4	3	3	1	5	2	8	5+
Warrior	4	4	3	3	1	5	1	8	5+
Reaver	4	4	4	4	1	6	1	8	4+
Reaver Succubus	4	4	4	4	1	6	2	8	4+
Hellion	4	4	3	3	1	6	1	8	5+
Hellion Succubus	4	4	3	3	1	6	2	8	5+
Scourge	4	4	3	3	1	5	1	8	5+
Talos	5	3	7	7	3	4	D6	n/a	3+

	Armour			
	Front	Side	Rear	BS
Raider	10	10	10	4
Ravager	11	11	10	4

RANGED WEAPONS

Weapon	Range	Str.	AP	Type
Blaster	12"	8	2	Assault 1*
Dark Lance	36"	8	2	Heavy 1*
Destructor	Template	4	D6	Assault 1*
Disintegrator	max = 36"	7	2	Heavy 1 Blast*
	sust = 24"	4	3	Heavy 3
Shredder	12"	6	–	Assault 1 Blast
Splinter Cannon	24"	4	5	Assault 4
Splinter Pistol	12"	3	5	Pistol
Splinter Rifle	24"	3	5	Rapid Fire
Stinger	12"	n/a	6	Assault 1*
Terrorfex	12"	n/a	n/a	Assault 1 Blast*

These weapons have additional special rules, see the Wargear section of the Warhammer 40,000 rulebook for more details.

DARK ELDAR WARGEAR

The following rules describe how all of the arcane weapons and devices used by the Dark Eldar work during a battle. These rules tend to be more detailed than those included in the Warhammer 40,000 rulebook, and they supersede them if they are different. Any items not listed here function exactly as described in the Warhammer 40,000 rulebook.

Agonisers: These are close combat weapons that affect a victim's nervous system, causing such severe pain that they can disable or kill even the largest opponent. They come in a wide variety of types, but the most common are whips and barbed gauntlets. All forms of agonisers work as follows: roll to hit as normal, but don't roll to wound. Instead hits cause 1 wound on a D6 roll of 4+ regardless of Strength/Toughness, and no armour saves are allowed (invulnerable saves may be taken as normal). Vehicles hit by an agoniser take a glancing hit on a D6 roll of 6, regardless of the vehicle's Armour value.

Blaster: The blaster is a short-ranged weapon that works in the same way as a dark lance (see below). It has the following profile:

Rng: 12"   S: 8   AP: 2   Assault 1

Just like the dark lance, a blaster treats vehicles with an Armour value greater than 12 as 12.

Combat Drugs: Dark Eldar characters have access to a wide range of effective but potentially lethal combat drugs, which are dispensed automatically from a neurally controlled device. They may be taken at the start of any assault phase, and allow the character to choose any number of the options below. Roll 1D6 per option chosen. If a double is rolled on the dice then the model suffers 1 wound. If a triple is rolled then the model is killed outright. Yes, this means that you cannot be hurt if you only pick one option. Note that no saves are allowed against this wound, not even invulnerable saves. All effects last for one assault phase (apart from wounds inflicted on the user by the drugs, which are permanent!).

a) May make 12" assault move and 3D6 pursuit/fall back move.
b) +1 WS
c) +1 S
d) Always strikes first, regardless of cover or weapons
e) Re-roll any misses in close combat
f) +1 Attack

Crucible of Malediction: No one knows what arcane arts the Dark Eldar use to create their Crucibles of Malediction. Each crucible appears to contain the trapped spirits of psykers captured and tortured by the Dark Eldar. When released, these spirits hurtle across the battlefield unleashing a psychic cacophony that can drive an enemy psyker insane. A character carrying a crucible may use it in the shooting phase instead of moving or shooting. When the crucible is used the

nearest enemy psyker must pass a Leadership test. Subtract -1 from the psyker's Ld if he is within 12" of the model with the crucible, and add +1 to his Ld if he is over 24" away.

If the test is failed the psyker is removed from play. No saves of any kind are allowed, and the pysker is killed no matter how many wounds he has. If the nearest psyker passes his Ld test then the next nearest must test, and so on until either all psykers have passed, or one has failed.

A crucible can only be used once per battle, and only one can be taken per army.

Dark Lance: The dark lance fires a beam of dark energy that annihilates anything it hits. It is especially effective against heavily armoured vehicles, whose thick armour plate offers no protection against the beam. The dark lance has the following profile:

Rng: 36"   S: 8   AP: 2   Heavy 1

Due to its unique nature it counts Armour values higher than 12 as 12.

Destructor: This weapon is only used by the Haemonculi. It fires a spray of highly corrosive acid that can eat through any armour and has the following profile:

Rng: flamer template   S: 4   AP: D6   Assault 1

The Destructor does not have an Armour Piercing value. Instead, roll a D6 for each target hit to see what the AP value of the hit is (eg, a D6 roll of 3 would give an AP value of 3). In addition, targets hit by a destructor may not take saves for being in cover.

Disintegrator: The disintegrator fires a small particle of dark matter in much the same way that an Imperial plasma cannon fires super-heated plasma. It is, however, a much more sophisticated weapon and can be set to either fire a large bolt, or a burst of smaller shots. Before firing the disintegrator declare if you're firing it on maximal (one big shot) or sustained (several smaller shots). The attacks have the following profiles:

Maximal = Rng 36", S7, AP2, heavy 1 blast
Sustained = Rng 24", S4, AP3, heavy 3.

Gruesome Talismans: Many Dark Eldar wear talismans such as fingers, ears or eyes they've taken from opponents they have slain. Models with gruesome talismans count as two models when working out if one side outnumbers the other in close combat. Note that this works against any foe, including Daemons!

Haywire Grenades: The Dark Eldar use these grenades solely for one purpose – to cripple the control systems of an enemy vehicle. This is done by the short-ranged

but extremely powerful electro-magnetic pulse that the grenade produces when detonated. The grenade, however, first needs to be clamped in place before activated, which means that each model using a grenade makes only one attack and doesn't count bonus attacks for charging, extra hand weapons, etc. If you hit, roll on the following table to see the effect of the haywire grenade on the target:

1 = No effect

2-5 = Glancing Hit

6 = Penetrating Hit.

Haywire grenades can only be used against Dreadnoughts if the Dreadnought is already immobilised.

Hellglaive: Hellions are armed with a unique weapon called a hellglaive. It incorporates a splinter rifle and a set of vicious cutting blades that are capable of slicing a man in half as the Hellion swoops into close combat. The hellglaive can be used as a splinter rifle or a close combat weapon, but may not be used as both in the same turn. If the user charges into close combat then the hellglaive also adds +1 to their Strength for the first round of combat. The hellglaive requires two hands to use, so can't be combined with any other weapon. Characters taking a hellglaive must also take a Hellion skyboard.

Hellion Skyboard: Hellions soar through the skies atop bat-like skyboards. In game terms these are treated as jump packs, allowing the user to move 12" in the move phase whilst ignoring difficult or impassable terrain. A model riding a skyboard benefits from +1 to its Armour save.

Hell Mask: These are terrifying masks that generate an aura that causes unnatural dread. Close combat opponent's must pass a Ld test in every round of combat. Any that fail will need 6s to hit the mask's wearer.

Plasma Grenades: These grenades negate the effect of cover in close combat, so that models strike in Initiative order.

Poisoned Blades: The Dark Eldar frequently make use of poison-coated blades. However, they have to be used with great care in case the Dark Eldar end up poisoning themselves! Hits inflicted in close combat with poisoned blades always wound on a 2+, regardless of the victim's Toughness. However, this ability may not be combined with the ability of any other weapon in close combat (eg, it can't be combined with a power weapon's ability to negate saves, a plasma grenade's ability to negate cover, or an additional close combat weapon's +1 Attack, etc.)

Punisher: The punisher is a two-handed power weapon used by Dark Eldar Incubi. It counts as a power weapon but also adds +1 to the user's Strength.

Reaver Jetbike: Treated in the same manner as a normal jetbike, Reaver jetbikes are almost the same as the Eldar jetbike apart from an added turbo-booster. This may be activated in any movement phase, and increases the jetbike's move to 24" instead of 12". However, the model may not shoot or assault on the same turn the booster is used. When a Reaver uses its jetbike turbo-booster then its saving throw becomes invulnerable for that turn and the opposing player's following turn. If one model in a Reaver jetbike unit uses its booster, then all the other models must also do so. Characters riding a Reaver jetbike may only be armed with single-handed weapons, and may only use one at a time (they need the other hand free to control the jetbike). In addition they may not use a webway portal or Crucible of Malediction.

Scissorhand: The scissorhand is a close combat weapon only used by Dark Eldar Haemonculi. It has the same effect as two sets of poisoned blades, so the Haemonculus gains +1 Attack in close combat, and all hits wound on a 2+. See the poisoned blades entry for more details.

Shadow Field: Surrounding the model in a dark miasma of energy, a shadow field absorbs the energy of any hits inflicted on the model wearing it, making them almost immune to any damage. However, the energy field can become overloaded and cut out. A shadow field provides a 2+ invulnerable save, but if the save is ever failed then the field is destroyed. Shadow fields are rare, so no more than one shadow field may be taken per army. Despite having a 2+ save, the model is still considered as being *fleet of foot*.

Soul Seeker Ammunition: The Dark Eldar use captured wraithbone looted from the bodies of slain Eldar Wraithguard to create a special kind of ammunition that they use in battle. Models using soul seeker ammunition may re-roll any missed to hit rolls, and any cover saves that would normally be taken by the target are ignored. Soul seeker ammunition may only be used in conjunction with a splinter rifle, splinter pistol, tormentor helm or a hellglaive.

Stinger: This is a special type of gun used by Dark Eldar Haemonculi that fires a dart of very virulent poison into the victim's blood stream, causing them to explode! The stinger has the following profile:

Rng: 12"   S: n/a   AP: 6   Assault 1

The weapon does not have a Strength value as such, and always wounds a victim on a D6 roll of 2+. If the target is killed place a Blast marker centred on the exploding model and roll to hit other models using the rules for blast weapons. The attacks have a Strength equal to the exploding model's Toughness, and an AP value equal to the victim's saving throw (ie, models hit by an exploding Space Marine would take a S4 hit with AP 3). Stingers count as having a Strength of 1 if fired at a vehicle.

Terrorfex: The terrorfex is a wrist-mounted grenade launcher that fires grenades made from captured Eldar wraithbone. The effect this causes is to produce nightmarish, psychically induced visions that terrify the user's enemies. The terrorfex has the following profile:

Rng: 12"   S: n/a   AP: n/a   Assault 1 blast

Roll to hit as normal, but don't roll to wound or save. Instead, if one or more models are hit then the unit they belong to must pass a Leadership test or become pinned. Apply a -1 modifier if the unit is under half its starting strength, and -1 per model hit if the grenade hits **more** than one model.

Tormentor Helm: The tormentor helm is worn by Incubi, and incorporates a neurally activated splinter pistol that can be fired by thought alone. This allows the model to use the pistol even if he is carrying something in both hands (like a punisher, for example). This means that the model gains +1 Attack for an additional close combat weapon even when using a double-handed weapon!

Trophy Racks: Many Dark Eldar enter battle bearing trophy racks adorned with the decaying heads of foes they have slain. If a model with a trophy rack slays an enemy in close combat, he may chop off their head and stick it onto the trophy rack! This adds +1 to the model's Ld for the rest of the battle. Unfortunately chopping off more than one head doesn't increase the model's Ld any further, but don't let that stop you doing it anyway!

Webway Portal: This is a mobile form of the portal used by the Dark Eldar to link together places via the webway. It may be activated by the model carrying it in the shooting phase, instead of moving or shooting that turn. Place a spare Blast marker in base contact with the model when it activates the portal. From then on units entering play as reserves may be placed on the portal template instead of entering on the table edge. There is no risk of scattering or being killed when travelling in this way, and the portal cannot be destroyed. Once activated the model that was carrying the portal may move away, and doesn't have to remain in contact with it. If you have a webway portal in your army, you may keep units in reserve, even if you are not normally allowed to do so in the mission being played. If you do this then the troops may only enter through the webway, and if it has not been opened on the turn they become available to enter play, they must be held back until it is.

None can tell what the true aims of the Incubi are. On the surface their only need appears to be to excel in martial skills.

It is claimed that they battle with each other, to determine their position within their own ranks; the victor of each deadly duel is given the privilege of taking the weapons and armour of their opponent.

Some have even challenged the Dark Father himself, but whether they won or died, none can say. That they have some hidden plan, some unfulfilled agenda, is without doubt. Whatever their reasons, no Dark Eldar Lord is without a force of these incredible warriors to protect them. They guard as much against the machinations of those within the Kabals as attacks from enemies on the battlefield.

CHOOSING A DARK ELDAR ARMY

The most satisfying aspect of collecting a Dark Eldar army is seeing it grow from a compact force of evil marauders to a sizeable number of depraved raiders from which you can create varied forces for different missions.

WHERE TO BEGIN?

The Dark Eldar have some very effective squads, but they must be used in combination with each other to achieve the greatest victories. Choosing which of the many squads you should collect is one of the most important and rewarding decisions you will make as a gamer. This section will show you some of the options and provide guidance on how to go about collecting your army.

The primary focus of any Warhammer 40,000 gamer is to collect an army which can be fielded in battle. The number of different types of squad you can include in an army is dictated by the army list and the Force Organisation charts. Of these, the Standard Missions Force Organisation is the most basic and also the most flexible. If you collect an army with these squad allowances in mind, you will end up with a force which can be used in any scenario.

As you can see from the Standard Missions Force Organisation chart above, an HQ unit and two squads of Troops are compulsory. These squads are the foundation of your army and so are a good place to start collecting and painting. When you have an HQ and two Troops squads you can fight a Standard Mission, although a fairly small one.

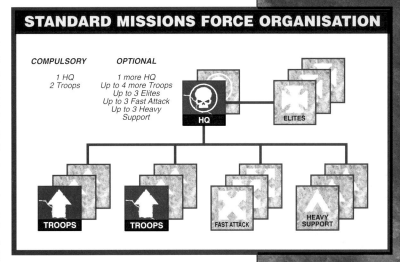

STANDARD MISSIONS FORCE ORGANISATION

COMPULSORY

1 HQ
2 Troops

OPTIONAL

1 more HQ
Up to 4 more Troops
Up to 3 Elites
Up to 3 Fast Attack
Up to 3 Heavy Support

HQ

ELITES

TROOPS

TROOPS

FAST ATTACK

HEAVY SUPPORT

Once you have your 'core' of compulsory squads you can start to think about the other types of squads you want to include in your army. By collecting a larger army, you'll be able to fight battles with more points on each side, and you will also have a much wider selection of troop types to choose from. You'll be able to tailor your army to a particular mission and opponent, and not have to take the same army for every game. Trying out a new squad in battle for the first time, and swapping and changing your army for each game, is what playing Warhammer 40,000 is all about.

Although an HQ unit and two squads of Troops comprise a minimum army, you'll no doubt want to add more! Every player has a different opinion about what makes a good army, and it's up to you to decide what best suits your style of play (and which miniatures you like best!).

You can talk to other players and read tactics articles, but there's no real substitute for learning about an army in the heat of battle. By playing games you'll learn what types of units favour your style of play.

To help you get started, over the page are shown a selection of the different squads from the Dark Eldar army list, with notes on what we consider their principal strengths and weaknesses.

A basic Dark Eldar force made up of two Warrior squads (Troops) and a Dark Eldar Lord (HQ)

☠ HQ ☠

INCUBI
STRENGTHS: Awesome in close combat, good armour, high Leadership.

WEAKNESSES: High points cost, cannot use Fleet of Foot rule.

HAEMONCULI
STRENGTHS: Special Haemonculi weapons.

WEAKNESSES: Needs supporting unit.

DARK ELDAR LORD
STRENGTHS: Good in close combat, wargear, high Leadership.

WEAKNESSES: Needs supporting unit.

↑ TROOPS ↑

RAIDER
STRENGTHS: Fast, Skimmer, carries ten models.

WEAKNESSES: Weak armour, Open topped.

WARRIOR SQUAD
STRENGTHS: Good Leadership, flexible, heavy weapons.

WEAKNESSES: Vulnerable to assault.

✠ ELITES ✠

WYCHES

STRENGTHS: Excellent close combat skills, combat drugs, special weapons.
WEAKNESSES: Weak armour, need to get into close combat.

WARP BEASTS

STRENGTHS: Fast, awesome when charging into close combat.
WEAKNESSES: No ranged weapons, weak armour, small units.

✗ FAST ATTACK ✗

REAVERS

STRENGTHS:
Very fast, good in close combat
WEAKNESSES:
Small unit, high points cost.

⋀ HEAVY SUPPORT ⋀

The models in this photo are converted and are not the actual Scourges available in shops.

TALOS

STRENGTHS: High rate of fire, good in close combat.
WEAKNESSES: Unpredictable, vulnerable to hvy. weapons.

SCOURGES

STRENGTHS: Deep Strike, jump packs, heavy weapons.
WEAKNESSES: High points cost, vulnerable to assault.

EXPANDING YOUR ARMY

Once you have an HQ choice and two squads of Troops, you have the start of your Dark Eldar army and can begin playing games straight away (albeit very small ones!). Very soon you'll want to start expanding your army by adding new units. As you've already got the compulsory units, you've got free rein over what to take next, although at first this huge amount of choice might seem a bit overwhelming.

It's a good idea to consider getting one of each of the unit types not already included in your army; in other words, get a Fast Attack squad, a Heavy Support squad, and an Elite squad. In addition, you should get at least one Raider to transport one of your troop squads, making them more mobile.

Any Warhammer 40,000 army will benefit from having at least one of each of these types of unit in it, so you can be fairly certain that whatever you get will prove to be a useful part of your army for quite some time to come. On this page we've shown our recommendations for good starting squad choices. Along with the starting force on page 17, they make for a good starting army.

◀ *In the sidebar on this page and to the right are photos of models we recommend for starting armies.*

After you've added a few more squads to your force and before expanding it even further, you should play several games with it. Once you do, you'll find yourself thinking "If I'd just had a squad of 'this' or 'that' in my army I might have won that game." Insights like this will help you to decide what to add to your army next.

You'll also find that you start developing your own tactics and style of play and this too will affect what you decide to collect for your army. For example, you might find that your favourite tactic is the *'Counter-Attack'*. If this is so you'll want to pick up more Heavy Support and Warrior squads in order to amass the firepower you'll need to make the tactic work.

On the other hand, if you prefer the *'Flank Attack'*, you'll be considering taking Fast Attack and Wych squads. Whatever your preferred tactics, very soon you'll have developed strong views about what models you want in your army, which will make collecting it that much easier. What's more, you'll also be able to have interesting erm... *debates* with other Warhammer 40,000 players about what makes up the perfect Dark Eldar army, as no two players are ever able to agree about such things!

Elites choice:
Wych squad

Troops choice:
Raider squad

Heavy Support choice:
Scourges squad

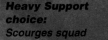

▶ *Fast Attack choice: Reaver jetbike squad.*

THEMED ARMIES

The method described above for collecting an army basically allows it to evolve and grow over time as you use it and learn more about it. However, sometimes very experienced players will decide to collect what we call a Themed Army, for want of a better term. The main difference between a themed army and a normal one is that the squads that make up a themed army will be chosen to reflect an aspect of the fictional background of the Dark Eldar race, and will usually be planned well in advance. For example, you might decide to collect an army based on the personal household of a powerful Haemonculus, with the Haemonculus as the HQ choice, a couple of small squads of Warriors as his 'personal guard', and loads of Grotesques and Talos for the rest of the army. Collecting themed armies like this requires a lot of experience of the Warhammer 40,000 game and so is not recommended as the way to collect your first army, but it's a lot of fun and gives you an opportunity to collect a really characterful army unlike any other. Whether it will win any games is another matter altogether, of course!

DARK ELDAR TACTICS

The Warriors keep up a continuous fire while the enemy approaches, weakening him before the counter-attack.

ON THIS PAGE ARE THREE DIFFERENT BATTLE PLANS WHICH UTILISE THE SPEED AND VICIOUSNESS OF THE DARK ELDAR ARMY TO THEIR MAXIMUM. YOU SHOULD MODIFY THEM TO SUIT YOUR OWN COLLECTION OF SQUADS.

COUNTER-ATTACK

• *Forces the enemy to commit himself, then hits him at his weakest point.*

• *Uses the mobility of the Dark Eldar to keep them out of harm's way until they are ready to attack.*

• *Good against enemies that specialise in close combat, such as Tyranids and Orks.*

When the enemy approaches close enough, the fast troops held at the back pounce forward and finish him off!

Each flank attacks first with its fastest troops to keep the enemy under pressure. The slower squads then move up to complete the attack.

ENVELOP

• *Uses mobility to surround the enemy.*

• *Gets the Dark Eldar behind the enemy so they can catch them in a crossfire and target the weaker rear armour of enemy vehicles.*

• *Good against armies without lots of squads to block the envelopment, such as Craftworld Eldar or Space Marines.*

Dark Eldar Warriors hold the middle ground to prevent the Dark Eldar being out-flanked themselves.

FLANK ATTACK

• *Use to utterly crush one flank of the enemy army.*

• *Concentrates the majority of the Dark Eldar against a small part of the opposing force.*

• *Best used against armies that are large and slow-moving such as Tyranids, Imperial Guard and Ork armies without too many bikes and buggies.*

The fast Wyches and Reavers attack first, before the second wave of Warriors and Warp Beasts.

DARK ELDAR COLOUR SCHEMES

All of the Dark Eldar Warriors and Wyches on these two pages were undercoated with black spray paint before painting.

Each Dark Eldar Kabal has a predominant colour or colours, which are generally used by the Dark Eldar raiding parties fighting for it. However, within each fighting force, the colours can vary wildly upon the inclination of its Lord – some have very strict uniform schemes, while others show little uniformity and are anarchic and varied. The Wych Cults are also each associated with a particular colour and all of the fighters from a Cult will use this colour somewhere. On these two pages are a number of different colour schemes for various raiding parties and Wych Cults, although there are many more Kabals and Cults than we could ever show, and you should feel free to invent your own if you wish.

SAMPLE KABAL NAMES	SAMPLE WYCH CULT NAMES
Bloodied Claw	Cult of Grief
Venomed Blade	Cult of Murder
Poisoned Fang	Cult of Violation
Rending Talon	Cult of Strife
All-seeing Eye	Cult of Wrath
Black Heart	Cult of Woe

KABAL COLOUR SCHEMES

DARK ELDAR MARKINGS

Dark Eldar Glyphs & Runes

Each Dark Eldar Kabal or Wych Cult is associated with a particular icon or pictogram, which often reflects its name. Such icons are used to display allegiance and are most often used on vehicles belonging to the Kabal or Cult, although important leaders sometimes wear them as part of their personal heraldry on banners, cloaks and so forth.

Dark Eldar waterslide transfer sheets are available from Games Workshop stores. Transfers are easy to use and can be applied anywhere you like on any of your models. Some of the available transfer symbols are shown to the left. You can of course invent your own symbols and simply paint them on to your models.

The Incubi and Haemonculi have their own colour schemes that are separate from the Kabals and Wych Cults. The Haemonculi are totally independent and their robes and armour are coloured to each individual's own tastes (though Haemonculi that have a special relationship with a particular Kabal may sometimes deign to use the Kabal's colour somewhere about their person). The armour of the Incubi is predominantly black, although the colours of face masks, trimming, piping or gloves can often vary.

WYCH CULT COLOUR SCHEMES

HOW TO PAINT DARK ELDAR

Choosing your force is just the first part of collecting an army. Once you have an idea what you want, you need to get some miniatures painted! This may seem a daunting prospect, but if you follow the advice on these pages, you'll hopefully find that it's easier than it appears.

An army of painted models is a great sight to behold on a gaming table, but first they have to be painted! Many gamers find it is best to paint miniatures in batches of five to ten models, rather than painting them individually.

Painting in batches has a number of benefits. Firstly, you can get into a steady routine so that you don't start from scratch for each model. Secondly, by the time you've painted a colour on the last model, the first model should be ready for the next colour, so you're not sitting around watching paint dry! It is also important to remember that you're painting an army to play games with – each model doesn't have to be a masterpiece! On the tabletop, the overall impression of a unit will count for more than any amount of individual highlighting and attention to detail. If you follow the steps below, you should be able to paint a perfectly acceptable Dark Eldar squad without too much difficulty and within a reasonable amount of time.

 ❶

 ❷

 ❸

 ❹

After cleaning up your Dark Eldar models and assembling them, the first thing to do is give them an undercoat. The best way of undercoating models is to use black aerosol spray. Spray undercoating is a real time-saver, as you can spray a whole batch of models in one go, rather than having to paint each one individually with a brush. Once the models are undercoated, set them aside for a while to dry.

Now you're ready to paint the first coat of colour onto your Dark Eldar. Using red paint and a standard brush, carefully paint all areas of the model except the helmet, splinter rifle and the blades protruding from the armour. Paint these blades, the helmet, and the blades on the rifle silver. Leave the rifle itself and the helmet plume black for now. Don't worry if you make mistakes, as you can always paint over them later.

Now you can paint the details of your Dark Eldar. Paint the armoured joint at the hips silver. Next, carefully paint the eyes of each model red.

At this point, you can base your model with sand, using the technique described on page 26. In the example above, the base has been painted Goblin Green.

Now it's time for the last few finishing touches. Use some light grey paint to pick out the raised edges of the helmet's plume. Finally, as an extra touch, you can paint another layer of Goblin Green on to the surface of each model's base, this time with a bit of white paint mixed in with the green, so that the sandy texture is slightly lighter than the rest of the base. Your Dark Eldar are now finished and ready for battle!

Although we've used red paint in the stage-by-stage example on this page, the same basic principles apply whatever colour you use. So for example, if you wanted dark purple warriors, simply substitute purple for red in the example above.

A finished squad of Dark Eldar Warriors, painted using the method described above.

PAINTING TIPS

These two pages detail a variety of different painting techniques that you can use to paint your Dark Eldar. Each can be used to obtain a particular effect, and with a bit of practice you'll settle on a style of painting that suits your needs in terms of quality balanced against speed.

Most of the techniques discussed below can be combined together, and as you will see, some work better with certain colours or on certain parts of the model. Like any skill, learning how to paint miniatures takes time and practice. Don't be afraid to experiment. Remember, painting is meant to be part of the fun of collecting an army, not a chore!

LOOKING AFTER YOUR PAINTS & BRUSHES

A workman is only as good as his tools, and if you try painting with a brush with bristles pointing in all directions, you'll end up with stray flecks of colour everywhere! To keep a good point on your brushes, always store them upright in a jar. When painting, use an old brush to transfer paint from the pot to a palette (a kitchen tile is excellent for this) so that you're not dunking the brush up to the handle into the pot. Also make sure you wash the brush regularly while painting to stop paint drying in the bristles.

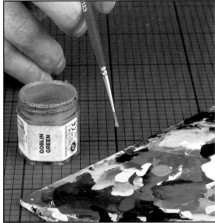

Citadel paint brushes come in a variety of different sizes, from a fine detail brush up to a large drybrush. Most of your painting can probably be done with a standard brush and a detail brush, although you may find a basecoat brush better for painting broad areas such as armour. A fine detail brush can be used once you've had some practice and want to try painting things like eyes and other tiny details! The special drybrushes are made of stiffer fibres, and are used for painting things like metal areas and hair or fur, as they don't wear out as quickly.

UNDERCOATING

Aerosol sprays are great for undercoating your miniatures – they're fast and give a smooth finish. When using sprays always work in a well ventilated area, preferably outside, to stop fumes building up.

A black undercoat is best for dark colour schemes such as black, dark green, or dark blue. Use white for lighter schemes like yellow, bright red or light blue.

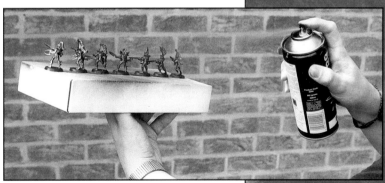

PAINTING METAL

To paint a metal area such as a splinter rifle, first paint it black. Get some silver paint on your brush and then wipe most of it off on a tissue so that only a residue is left. Lightly brush back and forth over the black and the colour will be picked up on the raised parts. More or fewer coats will change how bright the metal ends up.

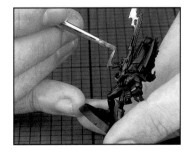

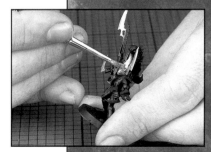

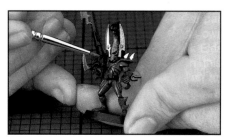

USING INKS

Inks are mostly used to provide a darker colour – adding shading to your miniatures. As inks are thin, they will settle in the recesses and flow off raised areas, creating instant areas of shadow when painted onto a model. Using inks in this way is sometimes referred to as an *ink wash*.

As you can see in the photographs above, inks can be used on armour (using an appropriate colour, such as red ink on red armour) and metallic areas (use Black ink, or Black ink mixed with a little bit of Blue ink).

If you have a steady hand, you can also use inks to paint a thin line into areas where armour plates join, hands meet weapons etc. This helps define different parts of the model and can be used to make certain features stand out.

You can also use inks on flat areas of armour to make a deeper, richer colour. The method for this is the same – paint over the entire area with ink and allow it to dry.

It is important to give inks plenty of time to dry, as they take longer than paint. If you put the next colour on too soon, it will mix with the ink and run everywhere.

BASING WITH FLOCK

You can finish off a base quickly and simply with modelling flock. Paint the base green and allow the paint to dry. Then paint on a layer of PVA glue thinned down with some water. While the glue is still wet, dip the base into a pot of flock and then shake off any excess.

BASING WITH SAND

You can also base models with sand. Paint the base with PVA glue and then dip it into some sand. Once dry, paint the base a colour that matches your tabletop battlefield. You can even paint a second layer over the top of the base with a lighter colour, for a highlighted effect.

Blades glued to underside of splinter rifle.

DARK ELDAR BLADES

The armour of Dark Eldar fighters is usually festooned with vicious blades and spikes. The plastic Dark Eldar Warrior models come with a selection of these which you can glue onto different places on the Warrior.

A few examples of where these can be placed are shown in the pictures to the left and below.

Blades glued to shoulder pad. *Blades glued to shoulder pad.* *Blades glued to arm guard.* *Long blade glued to forearm.* *Two rows of blades glued to arm guard*

RAIDER COLOUR SCHEMES

The Dark Eldar favour bold, striking colours for their troops and vehicles. As you can see in the examples below, a single contrasting colour painted onto a Raider's prow shield, runningboards or rear fins produces a simple but effective colour scheme.

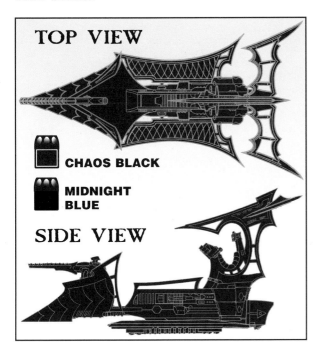

TOP VIEW

CHAOS BLACK

MIDNIGHT BLUE

SIDE VIEW

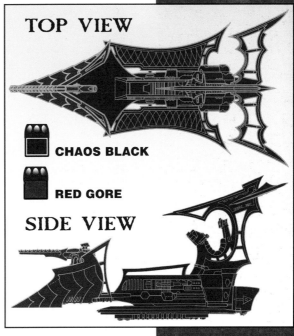

TOP VIEW

CHAOS BLACK

RED GORE

SIDE VIEW

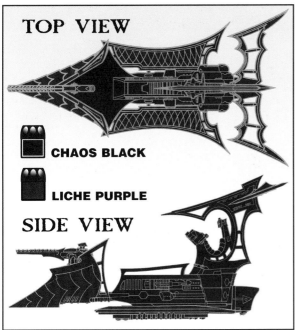

TOP VIEW

CHAOS BLACK

LICHE PURPLE

SIDE VIEW

TOP VIEW

CHAOS BLACK

DARK ANGELS GREEN

SIDE VIEW

▶ *You can also paint more complex schemes with different patterns and icons. Not all the vehicles in an army have to be painted exactly the same – by using stripes and other designs you can create a great deal of variation in your force using just a few colours.*

Many hobbyists find that painting Citadel miniatures is a rewarding and satisfying activity in its own right. On this page are a few examples of some superbly painted Dark Eldar. Whilst it would not be practical to attempt to paint an entire army in this fashion, models like these can form an impressive centrepiece for an army or, more likely, a dramatic and colourful display to decorate your games room!

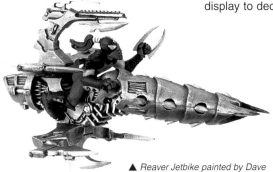

▲ *Reaver Jetbike painted by Dave Andrews. Dave has opted to model the clear plastic base of his Reaver by gluing small stones and other bits to it and then painting it grey to make it look as if the Jetbike is zooming across ruined terrain.*

▲ *These Dark Eldar Warriors were assembled and painted by Dave Gallagher. All three models (particularly the one in the centre) have been assembled in really dynamic poses. Their metallic blue armour was easily achieved using metallic blue paint with a coat of blue ink painted over the top.*

▶ *Dark Eldar Warrior painted by Martin Footitt.*

▶ *Wych painted by Anthony Bath. Anthony has removed the blades from the model's left hand and replaced it with a whip he's made from thin metal wire. The barbed tips of the whip are spikes from a Dark Eldar plastic Warriors sprue.*

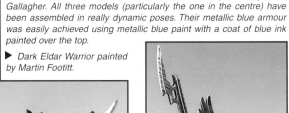

◀ *Urien Rakarth, painted by Adrian Walters.*

▲ *Dark Eldar Warrior painted by Gary Morley. The cloak is taken from a Warhammer Chaos Warrior Regiment plastic sprue.*

◀ *Dark Eldar Warrior painted by Neil Hodgson.*

◀*Beastmaster, painted by Chris Smart. Chris has slightly altered the pose of the model by twisting the torso around and bending the legs slightly to achieve a pose more to his liking.*

◀ *Dark Eldar Warrior, painted by Stuart Thomas. The mottled, shell-like look of the armour was done by painting small blotches of black onto a white undercoat and then adding three layers of green ink over the top, so that the blotches only barely show through the ink. The edges of the armour were then picked out with white paint.*

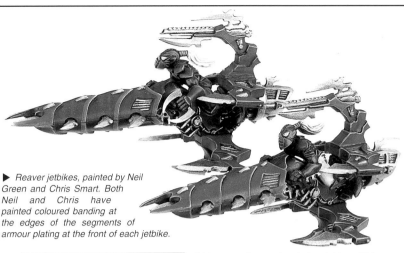

▶ Reaver jetbikes, painted by Neil Green and Chris Smart. Both Neil and Chris have painted coloured banding at the edges of the segments of armour plating at the front of each jetbike.

▲ Dark Eldar Lord, painted by Dave Thomas. Dave has used gloss varnish on the model's armour to make it appear shiny.

▼ Dark Eldar Lord on Reaver, painted by Ben Jefferson. This model has been extensively converted. The torso and hair of the Lord is that of a plastic Dark Eldar and the cloak is from a Warhammer plastic Chaos warrior. Numerous blades have also been glued to the Lord around his fist, on his skullcap and on his shoulder pad, all taken from a plastic Dark Eldar sprue.

◀Haemonculus, painted by Adrian Walters. Adrian decided from the start that he wanted to make the model look as gaunt and pallid as possible, and so mixed a lot of white paint into the flesh colours he used to paint the model's skin.

▶ Talos, painted by Richard Baker and Dave Thomas. The model has been painted predominantly black, but has had gold painted on the edges of armour plating, helping to emphasise the shape of the model, as well as acting as a striking contrast to the black.

The premier event of the year for miniatures painters is the Golden Demon competition. Part of Games Workshop's **Games Day**, the Golden Demon Awards see thousands of painters pitting their skills against each other to claim the prized Demon Slayer Sword. Split into numerous categories, from painting individual miniatures to vehicles and squads, the Golden Demon competition is the perfect opportunity to show off your skills.

Onlookers admire the many different Golden Demon entries at Games Day.

A force of the Kabal of the Black Heart

"Fetch me another plaything. This one seems to have broken"

Urien Rakarth,
Master Haemonculus

Urien Rakarth

A mixed force of Dark Eldar Warriors and Wyches

Scourges

Reaver Jetbike squad & Raider Transport

Dark Eldar raiding party occupying a captured Imperial garrison

A Dark Eldar force attack Catachan Jungle Fighters defending an Imperial Guard base

THE DARK ELDAR

In the following pages of Codex: Dark Eldar you will find a wide assortment of extra material on the Dark Eldar. It's not essential to read this if you have a Dark Eldar army, but you should find it interesting.

Included within this section are several special characters who are famous (or infamous!) individuals from Dark Eldar society that you can use in your Warhammer 40,000 battles.

Also included is a new mission, *Slave Raid*, to use with your Dark Eldar force. The mission has been designed especially to represent the main aspects of a Dark Eldar attack – to strike quickly, and inflict great death and destruction before vanishing as fast as they appeared.

Along with this there is also a collection of reports, rumours, and other background material, that bring to light the true ancient horror that is the Dark Eldar race.

Koradhil brought the biting blade across his foe's chest, tearing through skin and muscle in one fluid blow. Looking around him, the Exarch saw that his fellow Striking Scorpions had despatched the rest of the Twisted enemy. Gazing at the hacked and dismembered bodies lying on the ground, their vile blood soaking quickly into the soft ash dunes, Koradhil felt his anger rising. Why could they not accept the fate the Gods had dealt them? Why did they continue this pointless, futile battle against a destiny preordained many millennia ago? Why did so much blood, from Eldar and from others, have to be spilt for them to continue their depraved, unworthy lives? Gripping his weapons tightly, the Exarch gathered his squad and led them towards the enemy.

"Why do they resist?" Barakhar's ragged voice made his assistants twitch in fear. His wrath was dangerous, even lethal, and now that the battle was turning against the Dark Eldar his followers were even more nervous. It was Araqir the Haemonculus who spoke, unafraid of the Archon's anger, protected by his position with the Kabal.

"They resist because they are foolish, sire. They resist us, just as they resist their own true selves. They are blinded to the truth. They have seen the vile, ugly beasts that run ruinous across our kingdoms and they have bowed their heads to them. They lock themselves in that soulless prison they call their home and deny themselves the pleasures and pains that are their rightful heritage. They have lost the right to rule, yet in their jealousy they cannot allow themselves to stand aside while we take what is ours."

The Archon turned his face towards the Haemonculi. Behind the grimacing devil-faced mask, it was impossible to tell the Lord's true expression. The retinue waited in anticipation of their master's reaction.

"As ever, Araqir speaks words of wisdom. Well, if they will not stand aside, they must be laid low, with their guts open to the carrion and their eyes without sight. Send for my Incubi, announce the attack!"

"Keep watchful, my kin." Koradhil warned his squad. They nodded in agreement, and as they stalked forward their weapons were held ready to strike in a heartbeat. Suddenly a keening noise sounded in the air and as Koradhil's head snapped round to locate the source of the noise, a dark craft flew over the crest of a hill, it's heavy weapon sending a hail of dark energy bolts scything through the Striking Scorpions. As his squad was sent ducking and diving from the fusillade, heavily-armoured warriors jumped from the enemy transport. Koradhil recognised them immediately - the Fallen Warriors, the depraved followers of the Dark Father who had turned from the Light to the Shadows. Fuelled by a boiling hatred, Koradhil launched himself at the Incubi, his mandiblasters sending arcs of power coruscating over his armoured foes.

Barakhar watched his Incubi fighting against the forsaken fools of the Craftworld. Their weapons blazing with ancient energies, they slashed a bloodied trail of glorious destruction. The Aspect Warriors fought back fiercely, and the Archon could feel the surging waves of their anger and bitter hatred — their enmity only served to invigorate him further. He watched as Zharu battled in single combat with the leader of the enemy squad. Their weapons flashed and spun in a dazzling display of martial skills, each ducking and weaving as if in some complex dance. Then Zharu saw his opening and with a sweeping backhand blow sliced across the Exarch's neck. The Incubi leader's triumphant howl echoed across the battlefield as one of his minions picked up the Eldar's head and held it aloft.

Barakhar laughed fiercely. The Archons' foes were in full retreat, stunned by the ferocity of the counter-attack. Now nothing stood between his magnificent warriors and their real prey — the ugly, squalid conglomeration of metal and stone that the humans called a Hive city.

WEAPONS OF THE DARK ELDAR

CLOSE COMBAT WEAPONS

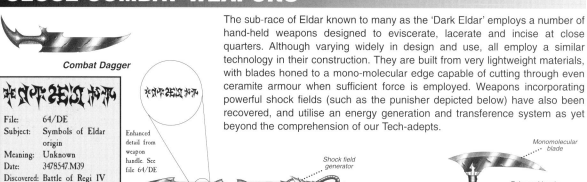

Combat Dagger

File:	64/DE
Subject:	Symbols of Eldar origin
Meaning:	Unknown
Date:	3478547.M39
Discovered:	Battle of Regi IV
Source:	Weapon recovered from body of Eldar pirate

Enhanced detail from weapon handle. See file 64/DE

The sub-race of Eldar known to many as the 'Dark Eldar' employs a number of hand-held weapons designed to eviscerate, lacerate and incise at close quarters. Although varying widely in design and use, all employ a similar technology in their construction. They are built from very lightweight materials, with blades honed to a mono-molecular edge capable of cutting through even ceramite armour when sufficient force is employed. Weapons incorporating powerful shock fields (such as the punisher depicted below) have also been recovered, and utilise an energy generation and transference system as yet beyond the comprehension of our Tech-adepts.

Monomolecular blade

Shock field generator

Polymorphic grip

Punisher

Extensible haft

SPLINTER WEAPONS

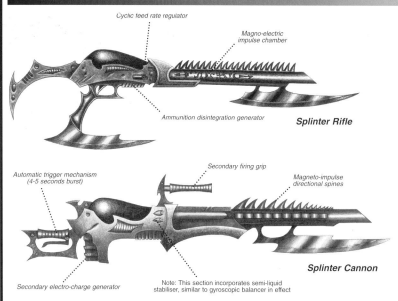

Cyclic feed rate regulator

Magno-electric impulse chamber

Ammunition disintegration generator

Splinter Rifle

Secondary firing grip

Automatic trigger mechanism (4-5 seconds burst)

Magneto-impulse directional spines

Secondary electro-charge generator

Note: This section incorporates semi-liquid stabiliser, similar to gyroscopic balancer in effect

Splinter Cannon

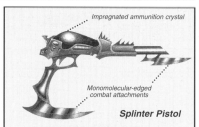

Impregnated ammunition crystal

Monomolecular-edged combat attachments

Splinter Pistol

A smaller version of the splinter rifle is the splinter pistol. It is often carried as a side arm by assault and shock troops and the only disadvantage of its smaller size is a more limited effective range. Splinter pistols and other splinter weapons are often fitted with vicious combat blades, which the Dark Eldar use to slash and stab opponents in close combat.

The standard armament of Eldar pirates is the so-called splinter rifle. This gun derives its name from its ammunition, as it fires a hail of splinter-like shards at the enemy. A highly sophisticated magno-electric impulse is used to break the ammunition crystal into small fragments, which are then propelled along the barrel at incredible speed with the same energy pulse. Often the ammunition crystal is impregnated with various toxic substances, and even a small surface wound can often fester, leading to considerable injury and pain. The splinter cannon is the most murderous of splinter weapons. With its highly efficient firing mechanism and lack of recoil, the splinter cannon can be fired by a warrior even when on the move, making it an excellent weapon for supporting the fast-moving pirate raiding parties.

'Though the artifices of evil are many, a bolter round kills just as assuredly.'

Inquisitor Skorn

HEAVY WEAPONS

Like all Eldar technology, the heavy weaponry that is employed by pirate raiders utilises an order of technology far different from our own. The dark lance is comparable in its role to that of the standard issue Imperial lascannon – that is to say, its primary function is to destroy heavily armoured targets. However, the dark lance does not employ standard laser technology as we know it, but instead fires a stream of what is, for want of a better term, 'dark matter'. The origin of this substance is unknown, although there are a number of theses claiming it can be found in black holes, warp storms and other celestial phenomena of great magnitude. This dark matter works by reacting catastrophically with its target, producing a blast that is more than capable of destroying any vehicle regardless of the thickness of its armour, or totally vapourising a foot soldier.

The disintegrator employs a more unstable form of this dark matter and battlefield reports show that it can be used in several firing modes, unleashing a single ball of ravening energy or a lethal salvo of powerful energy bolts.

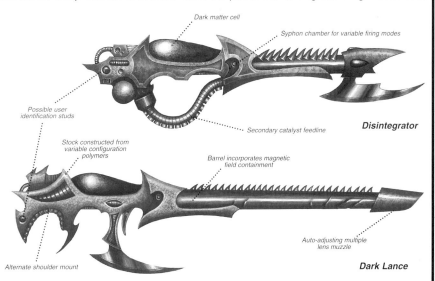

Dark matter cell

Syphon chamber for variable firing modes

Possible user identification studs

Secondary catalyst feedline

Disintegrator

Stock constructed from variable configuration polymers

Barrel incorporates magnetic field containment

Auto-adjusting multiple lens muzzle

Alternate shoulder mount

Dark Lance

SPECIAL WEAPONS

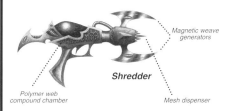

Magnetic weave generators

Shredder

Polymer web compound chamber

Mesh dispenser

There are a number of weapons entirely unique to Eldar pirates, although they often draw upon technology found in the weaponry of the Eldar of the Craftworlds. The shredder unleashes a web or mesh of monofilament wire, often with minuscule barbs or serrations along its lines. This mesh entangles the victim, slicing them to pieces as they struggle. Its dense cloud is also highly effective at finding weak points in a vehicle's armour, but is thankfully short ranged.

The destructor fires a stream of virulent organo-acidic compounds, which can melt through armour and sear flesh. The effects of these toxins can include blood vessel explosion or implosion; pharyngal contraction; extensive haemolysis; skeletal disintegration; sclerotic corrosion; intercostal spasms; hyper-reacted thermoreceptors and chemoreceptors; Eustachian damage; retinal scarring; cardiac and respiratory atrophy and aqueous humour deprivation. In simple terms, the victims are hideously blinded and disorientated, their skin feels as if it is burning, their respiration and even the circulation of their blood is erratic and extremely painful.

Translator's Note

Main device employed is debased form of Eldar Rune Atherakhia – 'Destruction'. Inscription believed to read "Bring about destruction of great potential to the ones who are opposed to the bearer", or words to that effect.

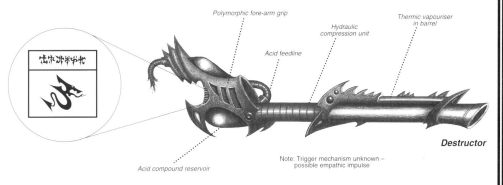

Polymorphic fore-arm grip

Hydraulic compression unit

Thermic vapouriser in barrel

Acid feedline

Acid compound reservoir

Note: Trigger mechanism unknown – possible empathic impulse

Destructor

ASDRUBAEL VECT, SUPREME LORD OF THE KABAL OF THE BLACK HEART

File: DE/4695/653
Classification: 2/a/de
Date Stored: 4784373.M39
Sub-section: Imp 272
Section: Alien/DE 45b
Warning: Not Sealed
Access: Authorised only
Validity: Unknown
Station Sent: Unknown

"I am truly disappointed that cruel fate has placed us in this position, such that I really have no choice other than to unleash my warriors against your population centres. If only you would lay aside these foolish hopes of protecting your resources and return to your homes and families, much bloodshed and woe could be avoided.

Yet... there is still time, any who leave now will be spared and I give you my word that they will be granted free passage through the wastes. This offer of amnesty will stand for two of your hours before the terror begins anew. I can only hope that you consider your position carefully. Send forth a representative to discuss further terms if you wish, or several if you cannot trust one of your number to speak for the rest. I feel sure that all can be... accommodated."

Comm recording discovered at the Delta 9 massacre.

"... therefore my studies lead me to believe that, with the exception of the Haemonculi, all Dark Eldar are members of a Kabal or Cult. The nature of Cults is dealt with in the companion volume to this work (Dark Eldar Cults Of The Thirty-Ninth And Fortieth Millennia), so I will confine myself solely to the Kabals of the Dark Eldar here. (Haemonculi will be dealt with in a future volume).

As already noted, Dark Eldar society is riven with strife, discord and murder, and any member of this society requires some form of protection in order to survive. The Kabals offer this protection to their members. Each Kabal is ruled by an overlord, and he has reached this position of supreme power through a combination of political intrigue, intimidation, battlefield prowess, skullduggery, assassination, and outright brutal murder. Such is the nature of the Dark Eldar psyche and character that the ruler of a Kabal has far more to worry about from his immediate subordinates than he does from any external forces.

This said, the different Kabals constantly vie with each other for territory and political power and it seems very likely that each Kabal controls a territory within Commorragh. There are certainly a substantial number of accounts dealing with street warfare between rival Kabals that would seem to back this up. For the ruling elite, however, conflict tends to be confined to the political and social arena rather than outright warfare, but even at these levels death and murder are often employed to settle disagreements between different Kabals."

Excerpt from the introduction to 'Enemies Of The Imperium: Dark Eldar Kabals Of The Thirty-Ninth And Fortieth Millennia' by Scribe P. B. Oschprey.

ASDRUBAEL VECT

| | | | | | Armour | | | | |
	Points	WS	BS	S	Front	Side	Rear	I	A
Asdrubael	277	6	6	4	14/11	14/11	14/10	7	5

Asdrubael can join an army from the Kabal of the Black Heart, so long as it is at least 2,000 points strong. If you take him then he counts as one of the army's HQ choices. He must be used exactly as described below, and may not be given any extra equipment from the Dark Eldar Armoury. In addition, he can only be used in a battle where both players have agreed to the use of special characters.

Wargear: Dais of Destruction.

Dais of Destruction: Asdrubael rides upon a Ravager that has been heavily modified to create a suitably ornate form of transportation for such an important personage. Asdrubael, Dais and bodyguard have all been given a single profile that reflects their overall combat ability. Opponents may not target individual 'bits' of the Dais, but by the same token Asdrubael and his bodyguard cannot dismount. As long as you think of Asdrubael, the Dais and the rest of his entourage as a special type of Ravager you won't go far wrong! The following rules for Asdrubael, the Dais and his bodyguard apply:

Type: Fast, Skimmer, Open-topped.

Energy Field: The Dais is protected by a unique energy field that gives it an Armour value of 14 in all directions against shooting attacks. Close combat attacks are made against the Dais' ordinary Armour values of 11 to the front and sides, and 10 to the rear.

Firepower: The Dais has two disintegrators and a dark lance. In addition, Asdrubael and his two bodyguards are armed with splinter pistols and they shoot in the same manner as models mounted on an open-topped skimmer. All weapons have a BS of 6.

Close Combat: If the Dais moved 12" or less in the movement phase, it may make an assault move of up to 6" if it is within 6" of an enemy model. The Dais fights in close combat in the same way as a Dreadnought, using the characteristics given in the above profile, although in this case the attacks represent the attacks made by Asdrubael and his bodyguard. Extra attacks for models equipped with two close combat weapons are included in the profile and should not be taken again. However, as Asdrubael and his bodyguard are armed with power weapons, no armour saves are allowed against wounds inflicted by them in close combat. Note that because Asdrubael and the Dais are treated as a vehicle they will **never** fall back, even if defeated in close combat.

SPECIAL RULE

Independent Character: Asdrubael is an independent character and follows all the Independent Character special rules as given in the Warhammer 40,000 rulebook. He will **never** join another unit.

+++DOWNLOAD COMPLETE+++
+++ELDAR PIRATE "KRUELLAGH" BIOPIC+++
REF: KTV651//019-6712 alpha
RESEARCH HISTORICUS: Scribe Parchett
'Information Is Power'
TAROT MATRIX: The Ravager Hides In Darkness

SUBJECT INFORMATION:
Name: Archon Kruellagh
Affiliation: Kabal Of The Flayed Skull
Honorific/Aliases: The Vile, The Mistress Of Skulls,
The Emasculator, Da Skinna, Mistress Hell-Fury
First Recorded Imperial Encounter: 6129967.M38
Status: Active
Location: Unknown
Threat Level: Very High
Recommended Policy: Extermination With Extreme Prejudice

EYE-WITNESS DESCRIPTION:

Witness: Cpl Anton Mossman,
Imperial Guard, 87th Blue Blood Regiment

"They came out of nowhere. Emperor save me, it hurts... I'm dying, aren't I!" [Interrogator repeats question.] "Yes, yes, I'll tell you, damn your eyes. They came out of nowhere... she led them in, that she-bitch from hell." [Sounds of coughing and retching.] "She was tall and, by the Primarchs, she was beautiful. Hard and lithe, and deadly swift... She cut a bloody path through us, and laughed as she did it... That laughter, it chills me still. She... she had this weapon that... sucked the life out of anyone she hit with it... they were left like dry husks, she sucked them dry and cast them aside... She revelled in their pain, it filled her... filled her with fury, made her faster, more dangerous... more evil... more evil than any living thing I've ever seen. Emperor save me. She was the death of me..." [Unintelligible muttering as subject slips into delirium.]

END DOWNLOAD+++
END DOWNLOAD++++++

KRUELLAGH THE VILE

	Points	WS	BS	S	T	W	I	A	Ld	Sv
Kruellagh	125	6	6	3	3	3	7	3(4)	9	5+

A Dark Eldar army from the Kabal of the Flayed Skull may be joined by Kruellagh. If you decide to take her then she counts as one of the HQ choices for the army. She must be used exactly as described below, and may not be given any additional equipment from the Dark Eldar Armoury. She can only be used in a battle where both players have agreed to the use of special characters.

Wargear: Hell mask, terrorfex (with Damnation grenades) & *Soul Flayer*.

SPECIAL RULES

Soul Flayer: Kruellagh is armed with a unique weapon called the *Soul Flayer*. From her hands extend two lethal spikes that can be used to impale a victim and extract their vital juices. The Soul Flayer counts as two sets of poisoned blades, so Kruellagh receives a +1 Attack bonus and always wounds on a 2+ (the +1 Attack bonus is already included in her profile). Any living model slain in close combat by Kruellagh, whilst in base contact with her, has his vital juices drawn off, adding +1 to Kruellagh's Attacks characteristic for the **next** player's turn only.

Damnation Grenades: Kruellagh's terrorfex can be used as normal or it can fire specially crafted Damnation grenades. When used to fire Damnation grenades it has the following profile:

Range 6"   **Strength 4**   **AP 3**   **Assault 1/Blast**

Independent Character: Unless accompanied by a Retinue, Kruellagh is an independent character and follows all the Independent Character special rules as given in the Warhammer 40,000 rulebook.

Retinue: Kruellagh may be accompanied by a Retinue of her finest warriors. These may either be Dark Eldar Warriors and/or Incubi, as described in the Retinue entry in the army list.

	Points	WS	BS	S	T	W	I	A	Ld	Sv
LELITH HESPERAX										
Lelith	110	7	6	3	3	3	8	3	9	6+

A Dark Eldar Wych army may be led by Lelith. If you decide to take her then she counts as an HQ choice for the army. She must be used exactly as described below, and may not be given any extra equipment. In addition, she may only be used in a battle where both players have agreed to the use of special characters.

Wargear: Hydraknives, falchion, razorsnare, shardnet, impaler, splinter pistol and shadow field.

SPECIAL RULES

Independent Character: Unless accompanied by a Retinue, Lelith is an independent character and follows all the Independent Character special rules as given in the Warhammer 40,000 rulebook.

Combat Mistress: Lelith is a master of all of the different types of weapons used by the Wych sect when fighting in the arena. She carries the full array of weapons and may use any two in a round of close combat (note that hydraknives must be used as a pair if you want their special rule to apply). You must choose which weapons she uses before any close combats are resolved. Lelith must use the same weapon combination for all the attacks she makes in a single close combat, but may change weapons in subsequent turns.

Wych Army: Lelith may only be taken as the leader of a Wych army. Her Wych army is chosen from the Dark Eldar army list with the following changes:

- Wych squads count as a Troops choice rather than an Elite choice.
- Warrior and Raider squads are Elite choices instead of Troop choices.
- The following troop types can not be used: Haemonculi, Grotesques & Talos.

Lelith's Retinue: Lelith may be accompanied by a Retinue in the same manner as a Dark Eldar Lord. If she has a Retinue it must be made of Wyches rather than Dark Eldar Warriors or Incubi. Each Wych model costs 10 points, and the Retinue may include up to 10 models. The normal options, upgrades and special rules used by a Wych squad apply to Lelith's Retinue. However, as the Wyches in Lelith's Retinue are an Elite force, you may choose which combat drug option they use, and you may include any number of models armed with Wych weapons (ie, you can take duplicates if you wish).

Designer's Note: Lelith can only be taken as the leader of a Wych army, and can't be included in a normal Dark Eldar army. This can cause problems if all you want is to add Lelith to your 'ordinary' Dark Eldar army. However, if you use the rules for taking several armies as a joint force (see page 131 of the Warhammer 40,000 rulebook), then you can take Lelith and a small contingent of as little as two squads of five Wyches each as an 'ally' for a Dark Eldar force.

"Never had so much alien blood drenched the arena. How could this be followed? The crowd cried out for more. There could be no end to the spectacle now. Then Lelith herself strode into the arena. The crowd hushed at the very sight of her beauty and elegance. Her flesh bared as if to taunt the blade to draw her blood. Her hair loose as if to tempt her adversary to grip it and strike the death blow. This was the way she liked to perform: so calm, so confident, so cold. The crowd gasped as she brandished her chosen weapons: a flashing of ice-cold silver, the kiss of death. Then the aliens were released into the ring. Not one, nor two, but ten assailants at once. Lelith danced with them, gifting each with a single choice wound. The crowed roared their approval, the entertainment would last long into the bloody evening!"

Dark Eldar Lord Sussarkh's recollections of Lelith, Mistress of Death.

DRAZHAR, MASTER OF BLADES

DRAZHAR										
	Points	WS	BS	S	T	W	I	A	Ld	Sv
Drazhar	90	6	4	4	3	3	6	2(3)	9	3+

Any Dark Eldar Retinue may be joined by Drazhar, who takes the place of one of the normal Incubi allowed in the Retinue. He must be used exactly as described below, and may not be given any extra equipment. In addition, Drazhar may only be used in a battle where both players have agreed to the use of special characters.

Wargear: Tormentor helm and *Disemboweller Blades*.

SPECIAL RULES

Disemboweller Blades: Drazhar is armed with a unique pair of weapons called *Disemboweller Blades*. These are treated as a power weapon that can cause 2 wounds for each hit inflicted (this means that 2 wound rolls are made for each successful hit). Drazhar's extra attack for being armed with an additional close combat weapon is included in his profile above.

Bodyguard: In the assault phase Drazhar may change places with the Dark Eldar Lord whose Retinue he belongs to. This represents Drazhar stepping forward to protect the Lord against an enemy attack. This takes place after models have charged into combat, but before any of the close combats have been resolved. The Dark Eldar Lord and Drazhar simply change places, and the close combats are then resolved as normal. Note that this may happen in either player's turn.

URIEN RAKARTH, MASTER HAEMONCULUS

URIEN RAKARTH										
	Points	WS	BS	S	T	W	I	A	Ld	Sv
Urien	100	4	4	3	4	2	4	2	8	5+
Uber Grotesque	+15	5	0	4	3	2	4	2	6	5+

Any Dark Eldar army may be joined by Urien Rakarth and he is counted as one of its HQ choices. Urien must be used exactly as described below, and may not be given any extra equipment. In addition, he may only be used in a battle where both players have agreed to the use of special characters.

Wargear: Destructor, stinger, poisoned blades & Crucible of Malediction.

SPECIAL RULES

Independent Character: Unless accompanied by a Retinue, Urien is an independent character and follows all the Independent Character special rules as given in the Warhammer 40,000 rulebook.

Master Haemonculus: Urien is a master of his craft, and the weapons he uses are amongst the finest examples of their kind. To reflect their superior quality Urien's weapons automatically wound if they hit – no 'to wound' roll is required. Armour saves are taken normally.

Retinue: Urien may be accompanied by a Retinue of up to five Uber Grotesques. The Uber Grotesques are chosen in the same manner as a normal unit of Grotesques and cost the same number of points, but do not use up one of the army's Elite choices. The Grotesques are hand-picked by Urien and are amongst his finest creations, and therefore have the improved profile shown above. With the exception of the improved profile they follow the same rules as normal Grotesques.

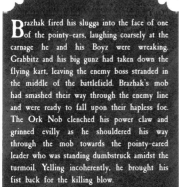

Brazhak fired his slugga into the face of one of the pointy-ears, laughing coarsely at the carnage he and his Boyz were wreaking. Grabbitz and his big gunz had taken down the flying kart, leaving the enemy boss stranded in the middle of the battlefield. Brazhak's mob had smashed their way through the enemy line and were ready to fall upon their hapless foe. The Ork Nob clenched his power claw and grinned evilly as he shouldered his way through the mob towards the pointy-eared leader who was standing dumbstruck amidst the turmoil. Yelling incoherently, he brought his fist back for the killing blow.

Suddenly, a blade came out of nowhere, slicing through his arm just above the elbow. Brazhak looked round and saw a tall pointy-ear, decked out in armour. Before he could bring his slugga up for a shot, the enemy attacked again, his lethal blades cutting across the Nob's midsection and chest, spilling blood everywhere. Feeling even his considerable strength leeching from him, Brazhak fell to his knees. Looking up into the mask of the warrior, his defiant glare was met by two pitiless, glowing orbs. Then the blades slashed back and forth one final time and Brazhak knew no more.

Deep under the cursed city of Commorragh, Urien Rakarth, master of all Haemonculi entered his secret laboratory. Here, in total darkness and infernal heat Urien worked alone, gibbering and insane. The walls of the laboratory were lined with captives given to Urien for his experiments. Chained and gagged, some were dead, some were alive. Of some, he was no longer sure.

Urien studied his prisoners, and finally gestured to his huge Grotesque bodyguards to bring one of them to his inner sanctorium. His choice was a muscular man, once a powerful Space Marine in the service of the Emperor of Mankind. Unable to struggle in the grip of the massive Grotesques and gagged with a snake-like organism, the man fixed Urien with hate-filled eyes. Urien ordered him to be tied to the operating table and then reached for his tools.

As one of Urien's razor-sharp claws drew blood the captive groaned. The luminous eyes of the mad experimenter lightened with a green glow as he felt pleasure at the man's pain. As he continued to work the Master Haemonculus talked to himself in a rasping voice. "You should be grateful. Once I remove your skin you will feel so much cooler. And when I have finished with you, you shall serve a much greater purpose."

Urien stopped and strained his mind to remember. Perhaps once there had indeed been a purpose, but it was all washed away now under an ocean of pain, cruelty, torture and insanity. Urien shrugged, and turned his attention to his experiment.

A cry of agony pierced the darkness.

DECAPITATOR, MANDRAKE CHAMPION

"And behold, there was one among them named Kheradruakh — He Who Hunts Heads — the Decapitator. A thousand skulls lined his lair; a thousand lives ended swiftly on his blades. None were safe from the Decapitator who moved through the shadows like the breeze through the air. No guard could mark his passing. No shield would ward his blows. None could stop him from seeking his prize. How could one name the price of certain death for any foe? I cannot say, but rumour tells of a hundred times a thousand given over in sacrifice, bartered for the death of a single enemy."

Tales of Terror III,
Geryon Publishing, Fourth reprint.

DECAPITATOR

	Points	WS	BS	S	T	W	I	A	Ld	Sv
Decapitator	112	5(6)	5	3	3	2	6	2(4)	9	5+

Any Dark Eldar army may be joined by Decapitator. If you decide to take him then he counts as one of the HQ choices for the army. He must be used exactly as described below, and may not be given any extra equipment from the Dark Eldar Armoury. In addition, he may only be used in a battle where both players have agreed to the use of special characters.

Wargear: Gruesome talismans, severed heads (counts as trophy rack), splinter pistol, *Additional Limbs* and *Decapitator*.

SPECIAL RULES

Independent Character: Decapitator is an independent character and follows all the Independent Character special rules as given in the Warhammer 40,000 rulebook. Decapitator will **never** join another unit.

Additional Limbs: Two additional arms have been grafted onto Decapitator's body. These add +2 to his Attacks characteristic and +1 to his Weapon Skill, both of which have already been included in his profile above.

Decapitator: This is the weapon that has given Decapitator his name. It counts as a power weapon, but if Decapitator rolls a 6 on any of his to hit rolls then that hit is counted as being at double Strength.

Shadow-skinned: The special chameleon-like qualities of Mandrakes allow them to blend into the background, even when they are standing in open terrain. Mandrakes always count as being in cover, giving them a 5+ saving throw against most attacks. This also applies in assaults, so unless the attackers are armed with frag grenades Mandrakes will always strike first. If attacked by something that ignores cover then their normal armour save of 5+ applies.

Master Infiltrator: Decapitator is a supreme master at infiltrating an enemy army. Do not deploy him using the normal rules, even in scenarios that don't normally allow infiltration to be used. Instead write down where on the table Decapitator is hiding (this must be outside both sides' deployment zones). You may reveal his location at any time by simply showing your opponent Decapitator's hidden set-up instructions. You must, however, reveal his location on your third turn if you have not done so already.

DARK ELDAR SCENARIO

Slave Raid is a special type of Standard mission that is played when Dark Eldar are present on the battlefield. If you roll a 6 when selecting a Standard mission and one player has a Dark Eldar force, then roll the D6 again.

On a roll of 1-3 follow the instructions for a *Change of Orders* as normal, but on a roll of 4-6 you must play this Slave Raid mission instead.

Both attackers and defenders use the Standard mission force organisation chart when choosing forces.

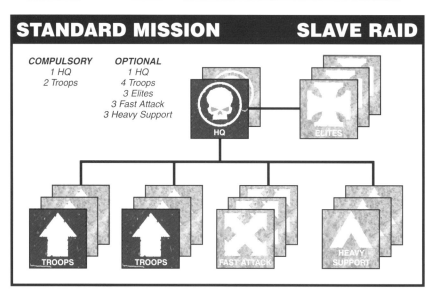

STANDARD MISSION   **SLAVE RAID**

COMPULSORY
1 HQ
2 Troops

OPTIONAL
1 HQ
4 Troops
3 Elites
3 Fast Attack
3 Heavy Support

HQ   ELITES

TROOPS   TROOPS   FAST ATTACK   HEAVY SUPPORT

The Dark Eldar are inured to terror and death, taking a positive delight in the infliction of pain and misery. Yet there is something that fills their race with an utter dread, driving them onto ever more despicable acts of wanton bloodshed and torture; the Great Enemy; the One Who Thirsts. What the relationship between the Great Enemy and the Dark Eldar is, it is impossible to say. Although the Dark Eldar revel in their own wickedness and evil, there is a desperation about them; an all-consuming horror that forces them to kill and maim each other, to fall upon their prey without mercy, as if their very survival depended upon the extremity of the grievous deeds they perform.

SLAVE RAID

OVERVIEW

The Dark Eldar make small hit and run raids all over the galaxy. They do this to steal and plunder or to simply cause wanton destruction, but most of all they do it to capture slaves. The Dark Eldar will steal slaves from any race, even Tyranids (Genestealers are much prized for use in the gladiatorial arenas in Commorragh).

This mission deals with just such a Dark Eldar slave raid. The defenders are not expecting an attack, and are spread out around their base camp. The Dark Eldar must move in quickly, capture some prisoners, and then escape before defending reserves arrive in strength.

SCENARIO SPECIAL RULES

Slave Raid uses *Reserves*, *Infiltration*, *Victory Points* and *Random Game Length*.

The Dark Eldar may choose to attack at night, in which case they may use the *Night Fighting* rules as well.

Dark Eldar units may leave the table in this mission. They do this by moving off the table within 6" of their entry point (see Set-up below). Once a Dark Eldar unit has left, it may not return to the battlefield.

SET-UP

1 The defender first sets up all of his Troops and one other unit of his choice. These are then deployed one unit at a time, anywhere on the table that is at least 12" from a table edge and at least 6" away from any other unit that has already been deployed. All other defending units are kept in reserve.

2 Roll the Scatter dice and mark the place on the edge of the table where the arrow is pointing to with a dice or a counter. All Dark Eldar units (except Mandrakes, because of their special deployment rule) set up within 6" of this point. Any models that will not fit on to the table can enter from this point in the Dark Eldar's first turn. Dark Eldar Mandrakes can set up within 24" of the entry point using their special deployment rules.

3 The Dark Eldar get the first turn in this mission.

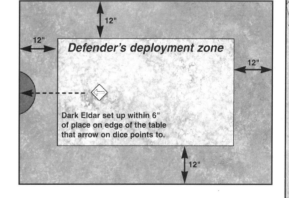

Defender's deployment zone

Dark Eldar set up within 6" of place on edge of the table that arrow on dice points to.

MISSION OBJECTIVE

The Dark Eldar win if they score more victory points than the defender *and* have captured at least one prisoner. The defender wins if he has more victory points. Any other result is a draw.

The defender receives 50 bonus victory points for each Dark Eldar unit, apart from Mandrakes, still on the table at the end of the mission. This represents the defender preventing Dark Eldar units from leaving with any prisoners they may have.

RESERVES

The defender's reserves enter anywhere along the table edge opposite the Dark Eldar entry point.

GAME LENGTH

The game lasts for a variable number of turns.

LINE OF RETREAT

The Dark Eldar must fall back towards their entry point. The defender's forces fall back towards the table edge opposite the Dark Eldar's entry point.

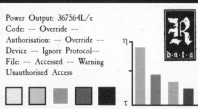

Power Output: 367564L/c
Code: -- Override --
Authorisation: -- Override --
Device -- Ignore Protocol--
File: -- Accessed -- Warning
Unauthorised Access

η

τ

R
d.a.t.a

CLASSIFIED
Subject: 8/3/Dark Eldar
File: 3474659.M39
Loading: 99.9% Complete
Authorised: Imp 457/b
Source: Imp/Inq/Psy/A
Access Code: TraceD

SITUATION REPORT ON ELDAR PIRATE ACTIVITY IN THE SPARTUS SECTOR.

Directed to: +++++++ Admiral Borghi, Naval
Command Station, Bakka
Orbit.

Commit to: +++++++ Imperial EP 343/72
Inquisition INR 2422/31

Crossfile to: ++++++ Alien Attacks [Al.At]

Transmitted: +++++++ Werarwe [Josh system]

Purity Check: +++++ Inquisitor Strictus

Input Date: +++++++ 5235723.M39

Compiled: +++++++ Mikael Spear, Assimilator
Minor, Officio Monitoris
Spartus Sector

Thought for the Day: Honour, Duty & Obedience.

Over the last three decades, there has been a significant increase in the number of attacks committed by the Eldar in this sector. This raiding activity has now reached the pre-determined level of tolerance as laid down in the Sectoris Stabilis Mandate [0125967.M34] and so the formation of this report has been instigated to bring the problem to your attention. The following are incidents which have reached a Threat Level of Delta-Majoris on the Sectoris Stabilis Mandate Magnitude Scale.

· [5218694.M39] Jericho system. Eldar pirates attack Jericho III, destroying the capital, killing 3,200 defence force personnel and 1,400 civilians, capturing 1,500 defence personnel and 16,800 civilians (±03%).

· [5354699.M39] Wilderness space - 152.6:91.7:31.5K. Remains of convoy en route to Vistro discovered. Imperial Navy Cruiser Judgement destroyed, 4 escorts destroyed, 12 Free Charter merchant vessels destroyed. Two destroyed Eldar vessels recovered for analysis. Shipment of ores missing, presumed captured. Shipments of technical materials and foodstuffs abandoned.

· [5685705.M39] Stratix Forge World. In a small-scale engagement, Eldar troops penetrated the polar arsenal, absconding with an undisclosed amount of experimental military hardware. Losses on both sides were minimal, but breach of Sector Security implicit in the nature of the items stolen.

· [5233709.M39] Banelund. Contact with colony on Banelund XI lost. Investigative team found all of the 1,200 colonists slain or missing, presumed captured. The attack on Banelund is prominent because of the previously undiscovered presence of an alien edifice on planet's surface, judged by Inquisition to be some form of warpspace portal, almost undoubtedly Eldar in origin.

· [5354719.M39] Jurn Orbit. Imperial Navy vessels clash with Eldar forces. Attackers driven off - loss of the Battleship Excessive Force, the cruisers Pious Victory and Mighty Endeavour plus 8 assorted support vessels. Eldar losses number 12 ships of undisclosed classification. The Eldar's disengagement from the warp within the normally intolerable circumstances of an in-system gravity field provides more proof of the Eldar's ability to appear almost instantaneously in orbit over a world.

The attached map also shows the location of incidents from a Delta-Minoris to a Gamma-Majoris Threat Level. I am sure you will concur with our evaluation that the majority of attacks seem to focus around an area of space at 153.1:91.6L:3L.3K. In your wisdom, you may find it appropriate to despatch a suitably sized punitive fleet to this position, either to locate and destroy any Eldar outpost that may be present, or to await the interception and engagement of Eldar forces in the surrounding systems.

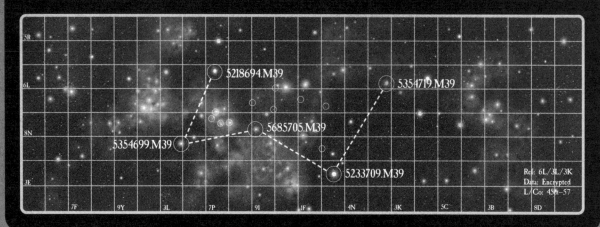

5R
6L
8N
3E

5218694.M39

5354719.M39

5685705.M39

5354699.M39

5233709.M39

Ref: 6L/3L/3K
Data: Encrypted
L/Co: 457-57

7F   9Y   3L   7P   9I   1F   4N   3K   5C   3B   8D

What can one say of Commorragh, the Dark City of the Eldar? It is the embodiment of anarchy and terror. It is fear, hatred and desperation incarnate. How long I was enslaved in that timeless city, I cannot say. There is no day or night, just an eternal twilight, an ever-present ruddy glow that bathes all things in blood-light. The air is filled with screams and cruel laughter. When they put out my eyes, my ears alone still conveyed that omnipresent aura of dread and loathing.

They took great delight in telling us what tortures and agonies they had prepared, using dread-ridden anticipation as another means to increase our suffering. When the Masters deigned to speak to us, they brought arcane machines to translate their words; they would not sully their tongues with the language of others. Most of my fellow slaves fell beneath the blades and poisons of those torturers beyond compare; the Haemonculi. Sometimes a Succubus of the Wyches would come and take the fittest to battle against brutal creatures and skilled fighters in the death arenas. Ten men at a time, great warriors amongst humanity, would face a lone gladiator. They stood no chance against the Wyches; who delighted in toying with their foe, slashing and cutting, darting to and fro, leaving a trickle of blood with every pass.

No-one dies quickly in the Dark City.

They prey upon each other as much as their captives. The great Kabals may hold power, but in the twisting alleys and dusk-shrouded corridors, allegiance is secondary to martial skill. To stray into the wrong territory is tantamount to suicide, running battles are fought every day, blood is spilt constantly. The ghastly Mandrakes are the worst, one wizened old slave told us. They stalk the shadows at will, plucking their victims from their homes, ambushing the unwary and slicing them to death with their claws. We were never truly imprisoned in the slave quarters, but it was clear that if we left, we would be at the mercy of the Dark City – a barrier more effective than any amount of walls, fences and razorwire.

They made no attempt to hide their deceitful ways, actually glorifying in treachery and betrayal. Assassination, murder and double-dealing are established ways of life to these decadents. Ownership of myself changed hands so many times that I was unsure who were my masters and who were their enemies. Some times I was stolen, other times I was traded for raw souls, given as a prize in the arena, or simply taken as a right of conquest.

Life is worthless in the Dark City, only pain, misery and death have value.

Others I saw, humans amongst them, who took to this depraved life with natural empathy. They bowed down to the Eldar and treated them as lords, in return for favours. It is claimed that the most promising are taken as apprentices by the Haemonculi. Most end up as twisted creatures in permanent agony, but others survive and learn, to be let free again into the outside world to spread their corrupt ways.

The Hellions are a constant plague to all, they race through the winding streets, blades shimmering as they randomly lop off limbs and heads with wanton glee. They gather for insane races; goaded by each other they attempt death-defying feats of aerial skill. Many die, and when one of the Masters dies, others quickly gather to feed upon the escaping soul. They fight each other, bite and claw if they have no weapons, to partake of that precious essence.

My escape was miraculous; the Emperor must have rewarded my undying faith in those times. However, though I am physically free, my body bears the scars; the many, many scars. Every breath takes me to a new plane of agony, every heartbeat sets my jagged nerves writhing with pain. I cannot see. I cannot speak. Most horrid of all, I cannot forget. Nightmares and waking visions plague me, the drip of my own blood, the cries of anguish haunt me.

No-one escapes the Dark City.

The Annals of Terror, penned by Lasko Pyre, posthumously pronounced Heretic
[died by own hand, 647.M34]

"From desolate Nahakra and wind-swept Brak'hir I bring you my tribute, my Lord, Master of My Destiny, Ruler of the Void. Five thousand souls to be yours, one thousand slaves to do with as your slightest whim desires. These are my gifts, the offerings of my loyalty."

Khirareq, Dracon of the Destroyers, stooped to one knee with her head hung in deference, the thick cloak hanging from her slender shoulders sweeping over the ancient mosaic floor. Around her, guttering lanterns made from the fat of slave creatures spat and spluttered, causing long shadows to flicker on the tiny tiles and the trophies hanging from the walls. As she waited for the command to rise, the young Dracon studied the scenes decorating the floor. The mosaic depicted the rise of the great Akhara'Keth to lordship of the Kabal. Bloody battles, assassins' blades and outright war within the halls of the Kabal seemed to play the largest part. Such was the way of Commorragh; just as it always was and should be. The weak had no right to rule. Her musing was interrupted by the voice of Zharokh Hierarch, the Lord's eyes and ears.

"You may stand, Dracon." The advisor's intonation of her title infuriated Khirareq. The tone made it sure that she knew she was inferior; that she was less worthy than the speaker. Fighting back a retort, Khirareq rose. Zharokh's time would soon come. Very soon. She turned her gaze to the Lord, enthroned upon a huge chair and surrounded by testaments to his power. It was claimed that the bones of ten thousand aliens made up the dais on which the throne stood. Rumour had it that every day, one hundred slaves were brought before the Lord and that the Haemonculi would create a cacophonous chorus of tortured screams and anguished yells, playing upon terror and nerves to create a symphony of pain. The Lord would drink deep of their spirits, one hundred souls ingested as one. Khirareq almost shuddered, thinking of the exquisite rapture that must follow such a sacrifice. If all went well, she would know such pleasures herself. Akhara'Keth leaned forward, his thin, twisted frame seeming tiny against the bulk of the throne. His rasping voice was quiet, but carried across the hall with strength and untold centuries of power.

"Your gifts are welcome, Khirareq of the Destroyers. The Kabal of the Bloodied Claw is strengthened by your efforts, you will not go unrewarded."

Khirareq flicked her gaze left and right at the warriors of the Destroyers who surrounded her. Her glance was answered by her Sybarites with barely perceptible nods and the flickered affirmation of raised eyebrows. With startling speed, Khirareq leapt onto the dais, grabbing Zharokh by the throat. The air was filled with flying shards as her warriors opened fire with their splinter rifles and cannons. Dozens of the Lord's bodyguards fell to the surprise attack.

Dragging her serrated blade across Zharokh's throat, Khirareq bounded toward the throne. All round her, the Destroyers and the Lord's guards exchanged volleys of fire, slicing through each other's ranks. As the Dark Eldar died, the air was filled with escaping souls. A roiling mass of blackness hovered on the edge of vision, the screams of spirits in eternal torment sounded on the edge of hearing. But, before she could reach the Lord, a whining noise emanated from the throne as hidden motors lifted it into the air, out of reach. Shocked by this turn of events, the Dracon was stopped in mid-stride. The hangings on the walls slid effortlessly aside, revealing hidden portals from which strode a score of Incubi. Then she saw a movement in the shadows and heard a sibilant hissing. A sound which could herald only one thing - Mandrakes.

From the dark recesses, the warped creatures leapt upon the Destroyers, tearing the Dark Eldar apart with sweeping blows from their hideous claws. The shadow-shrouded fighters were joined by the dreaded Incubi, whose glimmering power weapons cut down a warrior with every stroke. Soon Khirareq was alone, surrounded on all sides by her enemies. The Incubi leader strode up to her, and she brought her blade up to attack. With an almost dismissive stroke, her foe's own weapon lashed out, tearing through her wrist. With detached horror, the Dracon looked at her own severed hand as it dropped to the floor, still clutching her blade. Focusing her attention, she released a dose of elixirs into her blood stream and the spurts of blood and twinges of pain quickly subsided.

The Lord's laughter resounded around the chamber; a chilling, sinister cackling that made even the hardened Dracon's skin crawl with dread. The leader of the Incubi grabbed her long hair in one gauntleted hand and forced her to her knees. As her head was wrenched back, Khirareq felt a blade pressing against her throat and a trickle of blood sliding slowly down her neck. The ebbing and flowing of released souls slithered around the Dracon, drawn to her blood and fear. She could half feel their wispy tendrils sliding over her, probing gently into her mind. She felt like screaming, but she gritted her teeth and was silent.

In front of her, the Lord's throne descended with the sound of throbbing power-lines and hovered just in front of her. The Lord began to clap slowly, sarcastically, wringing out her torment and fear.

"Well, well, well! Khirareq of the Destroyers is a bold one. Bold, but unwise." The Lord's face turned from a wicked smile into a fierce snarl.

"You dare attack me, in my own chambers! Did you really think you could seize power from me so easily? There have been over three hundred attempts on my life, either from the assassin's blade, poison, contrived accidents or open hostility. Needless to say, they all failed, just like yours, and I must say this is one of the weakest attempts yet. You wish power? You do not truly know the meaning of power. At my command, a thousand warriors will fall upon each other in wanton destruction, just so that the single survivor may earn my praise. Out in the city, there are leaders of other Kabals who tremble at the mention of my name, fearing my mighty wrath. Whole worlds have knelt before me, entire populations have been slain for my amusement. And you think that you can wrest power from me!"

The Dark Eldar Lord's eyes glazed over, as he took a long, deep breath. Khirareq felt the spirits around her drifting away, pulled towards the gulf inside the Lord's own soul. The Lord's body twitched spasmodically as he absorbed the freed life essence of his followers, which was coalescing around his throne in a faint mist. As the spirits of the dead were consumed, Akhara'Keth's spasms increased and a thin dribble of saliva trickled from the corner of his slack lips. With a shuddering sigh, the Lord finished and slumped back in the chair. When he sat forward once more his eyes burned more brightly, his skin was less wrinkled, his hair darker with more lustre.

"Why?"

Khirareq was momentarily taken aback by the sudden question, but calmed herself in a heartbeat. She stared straight back at the Lord, looking deep into the ancient pits of evil that were his eyes.

"Because I need to rule! Because I saw you as weak. But you have shown me now what weakness really is."

"You need to rule? What do you know of needs? You are young, the Thirst has a shallow hold on you. I will tell you of need; a deep, unfaltering emptiness that grows larger and more demanding with every passing of the night. You have heard tales of how I consume a hundred souls a day. That is but the morsel to whet my appetite. A hundred times that number die every day to quench my desire, my need. Spirits unnumbered are distilled in agony and torture to the peak of exquisite taste to fill the chasm of my soul. Do not confuse needs with ambitions."

Khirareq steadied her heart, waiting for the deathblow that would surely come. She had tried, her pride was intact. Her only regret was that she had failed.

"Do what you will, I am not ashamed of my deeds. I have done what I wanted, as is our code, and I will not bow down to a Lord who does not respect that."

Again, the Lord's chilling laugh echoed around the table.

"You must learn how to exercise power. You must know how to deal with the silent Incubi, the shadowy Mandrakes, the gifted Haemonculi, even the battle-crazed Wyches and the mindless Grotesques. And you will learn these things, I assure you. Let us hope you are more successful at uncovering plots against me than your predecessor, Khirareq Hierarch..."

Eyes without life,
maggot-ridden corpses,
mountains of skulls.
These are some of my
favourite things.

Drachon Borkor

"234345.M33: Tonight is Devilnacht, the darkest hour of the century when all the moons block the light of our star. As our fathers and our grandfathers have taught us, and their forefathers taught them since the colony was founded eighty generations ago, we have shuttered the windows, barred the gates, set the guards and prepared our defences. No-one has yet replied to our plea for help, and there are but scant few hours left before midnight. The soul-eaters will come, of that I am sure. Some scoff and say they are but tales told by drunken old men who wish to seem wise and foolish mothers who want to scare their children into obedience. But I know the truth, I spoke to Jeremiah before he died and he was there the last time they came, and his body still shook with the fear in his heart.

I remember his words exactly, etched upon my memory by the rasping of his voice and the intensity of his stare. I know some thought him mad, senile in his antiquity, but they were not there to see him, to feel his hands gripping my arm so tight that it went numb. "Fear the Darkness. Believe not the sanctity of Light. Nothing stops them, not barred window nor locked door, not gunshot nor sword blow. No portal is closed to them and no mortal man can stand against them and live. Make your peace with the Emperor on Devilnacht's Eve, for you will not see All Saviours' Day. Leave town, do not return, if you value your life." I remembered then his harsh, racking laugh which degenerated into a hacking cough. His eyes turned so hard, like stone, and he pulled me close to whisper in my ear with his short-gasped voice. "They don't just kill you. Some they slay, but others they take. They took Mia and Farah and Jeboh and Garret and Felix and Belsta and all the others. Chains and whips, barbs and talons... Their screams haunt my sleep. Why did they spare me? I did not help them, I swear!"

He became fervent, adamantly denying any collusion with the Devils That Stalk Men. He slept then for a while, but awoke just before dusk on Devilnacht's Eve. I was still there, I knew he would not live another night. The fever, the ravaging disease that had somehow kept him alive to the grand age of six score years and three was reaching its end, devouring his body from the inside. He raved incoherently for a while and I bathed his brow in ewe's milk as Grandmother Fammi had taught me. He quieted and became lucid once again.

"Be not here tomorrow eve! Go! Go away, far away! Hide, skulk, crawl on your belly through the dense tangles of forest if you must, but be not here when the Devils That Stalk Men come. Your soul will not see the Great Emperor, they will take it from His light and devour it for themselves. The pain of your soul will mirror the pain of your body. They feast upon fear, they drink your terror, they delight in your impotency to resist them. They will come and all will die or be taken. That is the way of these things. They don't kill you! They don't just kill you..." Then he passed away, his last words a mere rattle to show the passing of his soul to the Emperor.

Now, it is near starset on Devilnacht and the moons grow large. Now I understand why Jeremiah was spared, when the cold wind grips me and I see the faces peering into the darkness on the point of hysterical terror. He was truly spared, even given the gift of elongated life so that he may live to this day, and no further. He was a messenger. The Devils That Stalk Men want us to know. They want us to fear them. And they will come, and they will kill us. But they don't just kill you...

Last entry, Journal of Marenza Balthus of Thangod Colony, Beta-Coplin XXI.